PELHAM BOOKS

First published in Great Britain by
Pelham Books Ltd
44 Bedford Square
London WC1B 3DU
1982

Copyright © 1982 Johanna Davis and
Overall Publications Ltd

All right reserved. No part of this publication
may be reproduced, stored in a retrieval
system, or transmitted, in any form or by any
means, electronic, mechanical, photocopying,
recording or otherwise, without the prior
permission of the owners of the copyright

British Library Cataloguing in
Publication Data
Davis, Johanna
Machine Knitting to suit your mood
1. Knitting, machines – Amateurs' manuals
I. Title
746.4'32   TT687

ISBN 0 7207 1298 X

Edited and designed by
Overall Publications Ltd
Photographs by Di Lewis
Typeset by Unigraph Ltd, London
Printed in Hong Kong

Contents

Introduction 6

Monday 8
The technique: the basics;
the project: a bandeau top

Tuesday 24
The technique: ridges for pattern;
the project: a simple sweater

Wednesday 38
The technique: shaping and weaving;
the project: a colourful tunic

Thursday 50
The technique: Jacquard patterning (with or without punch cards);
the project: a smart black and white dress

Friday 60
The technique: tucking;
the project: a warm outdoor jacket

Saturday 70
The technique: fans for flares;
the project: a sparkling party dress

Sunday 82
Review of the week and ideas for future experiments

Useful information 96
machine manufacturers
yarn suppliers
knitting courses

From the author

This is a book for anyone who wants to knit by machine. Its aim is to provide the reader with ideas that can be interpreted on any machine, easily and enjoyably. It should prove equally stimulating to the novice, the student and the experienced machine knitter, for the approach is essentially experimental.

Machine manuals can often seem daunting. This book has been designed to introduce you gradually to the basic techniques of machine knitting, helping you to become familiar with the potential of your machine for the construction of knitted clothes.

The only prerequisite to success, as far as the mastery of techniques is concerned, is the ability to cast on, cast off and knit without dropping stitches. Once these three techniques seem easy, the rest can soon be learned by experimentation and with the help of the machine's manual. The only other essential is that, before starting a garment, you count the rows and stitches per 2.5cm (1in) in a sample piece of knitting that establishes the yarn, pattern and tension for the garment.

The book is divided into seven chapters. The first six teach basic knitting techniques and suggest a basic garment, which anyone might like to knit, designed to suit the mood of a certain day of the week. Most people feel very differently about themselves from day to day and a change of mood is even possible between morning and evening.

On Sunday, all the techniques learned and experiments made are reviewed and suggestions are given for other ways in which you can continue your own exploration of the craft.

Be positive and optimistic; if you are ready to explore and experiment with your machine, and start to think of knitting as the construction of a fabric and the creation of a garment, then the possibilities become endless.

The reasons for wanting to use a knitting machine are many: with some it's economy and speed, with others it is neatness and the facility to work intricate designs. My main reason is the desire to create clothes that are individual, original and appropriate to a specific occasion and expressive of a particular mood. I hope you'll feel the same when you've read this book.

Introduction

USEFUL THINGS TO KNOW BEFORE YOU BEGIN KNITTING

The difference between a single bed and double bed machine
The essential difference between the two machines is implied in the use of the words 'single' and 'double'. The former has one bed (of needles) from which the knitting hangs and is completely visible; the other has two beds (of needles) from in-between which the knitting grows, not becoming visible until enough has been knitted to appear beneath the depth of the machine bed. However, here it is possible to inspect the progress of the knitting by pulling out the knob on the right and thereby opening up the machine.

The advantages of the single bed machine
Because the knitting is visible, it is easy to spot any mistake and rectify the error before it is too late. Also, being mechanically quite simple, the principal stitch variations and needle positions are easy to understand. This makes it an ideal machine for the beginner and novice.

Advantages of the double bed machine
Having two needle beds instead of one gives the knitter a choice: using just one of the beds, the two together, each one separately, or only partly separately. There are also an infinite number of stitch variations and combinations, some of which will be introduced or touched upon where applicable at a later stage in the book. To test whether you have grasped the principal differences between the two types of machine, cut up several old articles of knitwear and see if you can tell which was knitted on which.

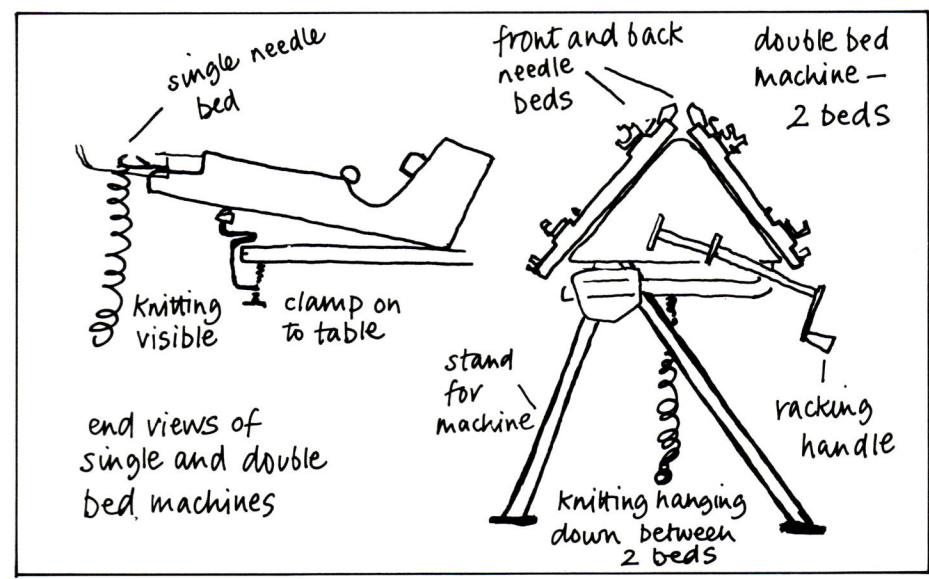

end views of single and double bed machines

Where to buy a machine
If you have no clue as to what type of machine you want, the best place to look is at a trade fair or in a department store. Here you will find a wide variety of machines being demonstrated, and this experience should enable you to decide whether your wish for a machine is serious or a mere whim. If the former, you can buy the machine on the spot, or having decided on the make and model you like, try to find it even more cheaply elsewhere. New and second-hand knitting machines are often advertised in knitting and fashion trade publications. If you find one through these channels of enquiry, the likelihood is that it will be in good order, that the seller can explain how it works and also direct you to where you can find further instruction.

Other possible hunting grounds are the advertisement pages of local newspapers, newsagents' windows and junk shops. Be warned, though, that in acquiring a machine from any of these places, you are taking a risk – unless, of course, you take a friend with you who is familiar with their technology. They should prevent you investing in any machine that is rusty, buckled, cracked, or has parts missing. If you are ignorant about knitting machines and have no one that you can trust, do not risk it: buy a new one. You can always buy a second-hand machine later on when you feel more knowledgeable on the subject.

Where tuition can be found
The manufacturers of all reputable knitting machines run instructional courses in their use and maintenance.

Usually these are freely offered on the purchase of a machine. If such a service is available, use it. You will find the advice practical and helpful, however limited and uninspiring.

Rather more stimulating are the courses offered to elementary and advanced students by art colleges and adult education centres. Standards will vary, so shop around. The same applies to knitting clubs: you will find them advertised in craft and knitting magazines. Of course, you may not want any of these things – just this book.

Where suitable yarns can be located
Owning a varied and inspiring selection of yarns is as important as owning a machine that works properly. One without the other is tantamount to useless. Begin by acquiring an assortment of yarns from a good department store. Study the labels so that you become familiar with the differences between wool, nylon, acrylic, viscose, cotton and silk. Make notes as to the texture, weight and appearance of all the yarns you collect. From the labels, you will soon become familiar with the mills and distributors of the various yarns. Write to them; usually they will oblige by sending you their shade card or cards. Visit them too. They are usually most helpful if you show interest and enthusiasm. Having discovered and explored their stock, order the yarns you require at half the price they cost in any department store or wool shop. Addresses of yarn sources, including lists of mills (further to those given on page 96), can be obtained from machine and hand knitting magazines, textile and knitting trade journals, public libraries, wool bureaux, cotton boards, fabric libraries and art colleges.

Creating a work area for your machine and yarns
Be serious in organising a space
The first most obvious requirement is a well-lit space, large enough to set up

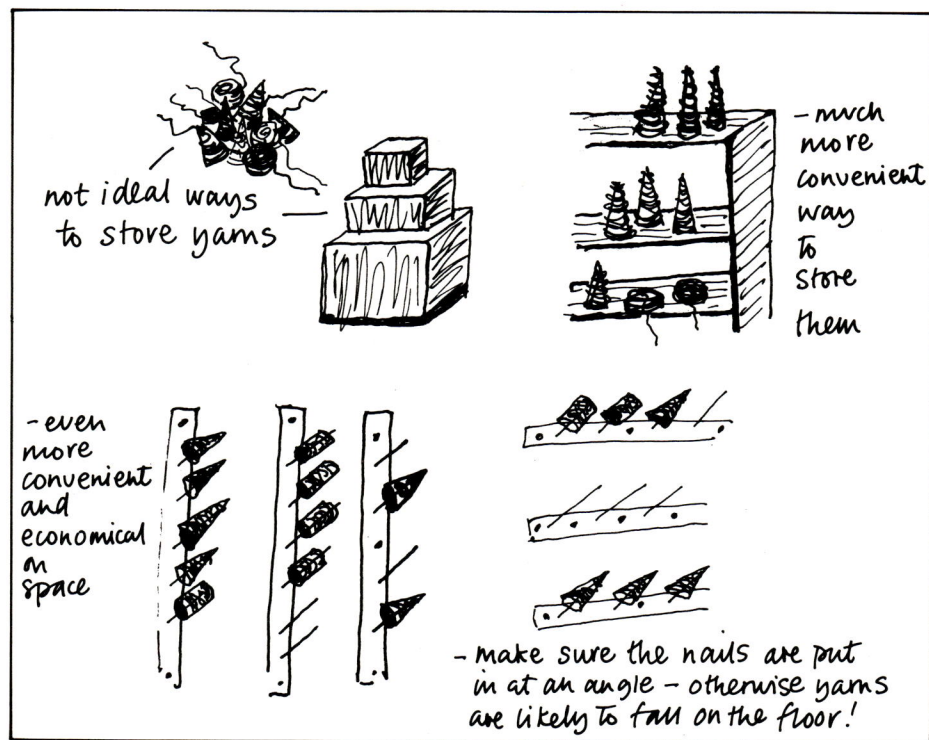

your machine, store the yarns and install a work surface. If the area is spacious enough, the machine will not require constantly being packed away and re-assembled; I suspect the bother of this puts a lot of people off machine knitting. However, I will assume that you are serious about the craft and have set up your machine for continual use.

Now think about storing your yarns
A pile of cones on the floor may look inviting, but is hardly practical. In direct contrast, a pile of cardboard boxes full of neatly packed yarns may be practical but is hardly conducive to creative thinking. Shelving of some kind is therefore essential, preferably not so high that you have to climb a ladder each time you want to try out a colour or texture. Neither should the shelves be so deep that the cones at the back are not visible.
Try screwing strips of wood bearing angled nails hammered in at 10cm (4in) intervals to the wall for the most economical way of storing 'cheeses' and 'cones' wound with yarn. Such a method takes little space, looks attractive and you can see everything you own at a glance.

The floor is not the best working surface
Much more convenient is a large, smooth-topped table. You will need such a space for laying out the pieces of a design for easy assembly of a garment and for checking measurements accurately. You will also need somewhere to sit, to write and draw up your notes, work out patterns, think or read. Besides, sitting at a table is a great deal more comfortable than sitting on the floor!

Now, are you all ready and prepared?
Hopefully, all this will have put you into exactly the right mood and frame of mind for the week ahead.

7

Monday

Monday is rather a fragile day! The most cheerful way to start the week – and your knitting course – is by making a series of bandeaux in mercerized cotton or a shiny cotton viscose mixture, either plain or finished with a fine lurex. These tops should make you feel thoroughly sexy and put you into a really good mood.

From a practical point of view, a bandeau is the simplest garment to make as a first project. Its construction is extremely easy: a rectangle of knitted fabric, with or without a seam or fastened with ties like an old-fashioned corset. It is also the perfect opportunity for constructing a fabric in which the stitch tension is exactly appropriate to the yarn used and you can concentrate on the basic techniques of casting on and off and perfecting your knitting.

The bandeau is also a thoroughly versatile garment, even when knitted in a perfectly plain yarn. Wear it in the summer when you are very brown, in the evening for a party, under a jacket, with a cardigan, trousers or skirt. By the end of this first day, you will have mastered some of the basics of the craft and have any number of bandeaux to wear. They should leave you feeling a great deal better than you did first thing this morning!

First swatch knitted on every needle with hem knitted first

Second swatch showing groups of needles knitting and gaps left where needles out of action

Third swatch showing rouleaux threaded through gaps in second swatch

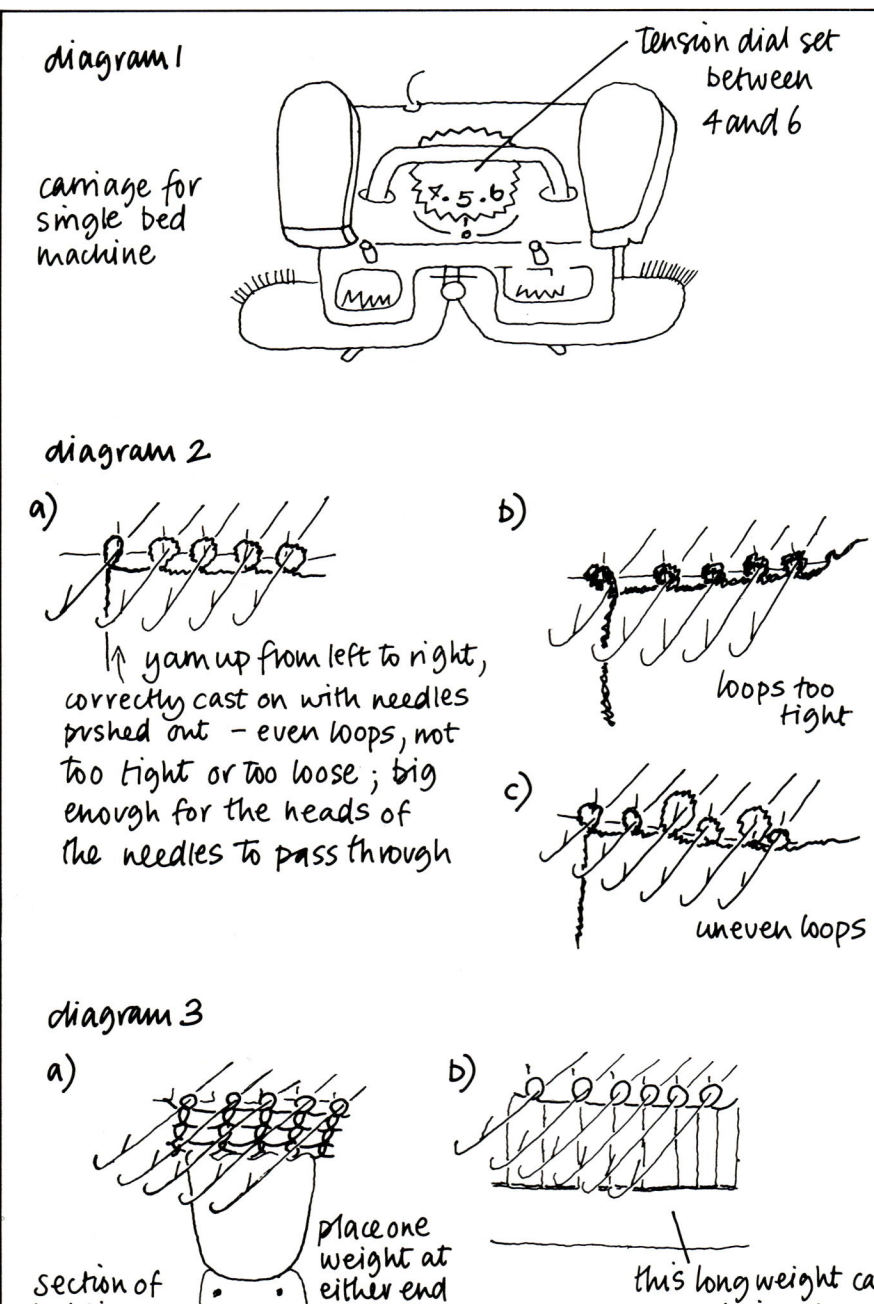

Diagram 1
Having set up your machine ready for work according to the instructions in your manual, set your tension dial at 'medium' for your first swatch. Most dials are marked from one to 10, so try between four and six.

Diagram 2
The next step is to cast 30 stitches on to your needles (a). It is important that you cast on as evenly as possible to make sure the stitches are neither too tight (b), too loose or too uneven (c). Having cast on satisfactorily, push all the cast-on needles as far forward as they will go, making sure your machine is set to knit in this position. (Refer back to diagram 1.)

Diagram 3
If, after several rows, you feel that knitting would be easier and the results more even with weights attached, secure them in place (a). If you have a long weight (b), you should have positioned this before knitting, so making it unnecessary to push out the needles.

Diagram 4
Having knitted about 40 rows, cast off your first swatch as carefully as you cast on, using the transfer tool provided (a). To keep the cast-off edge even, it is helpful to loop the yarn around the spike adjacent to each needle as stitches are cast off (b). This will ensure the line is straight as well as the stitches cast off evenly (c).

Diagram 5
After removing the swatch from the machine, lay it carefully, and squarely on an ironing board. If the edges are curling, insert pins horizontally so that they are held down flat. Some yarns are not suitable for pressing so check the ballband for fibre content and washing and pressing instructions and act accordingly.
Once pressed, you will be able to tell whether the swatch has worked or not.

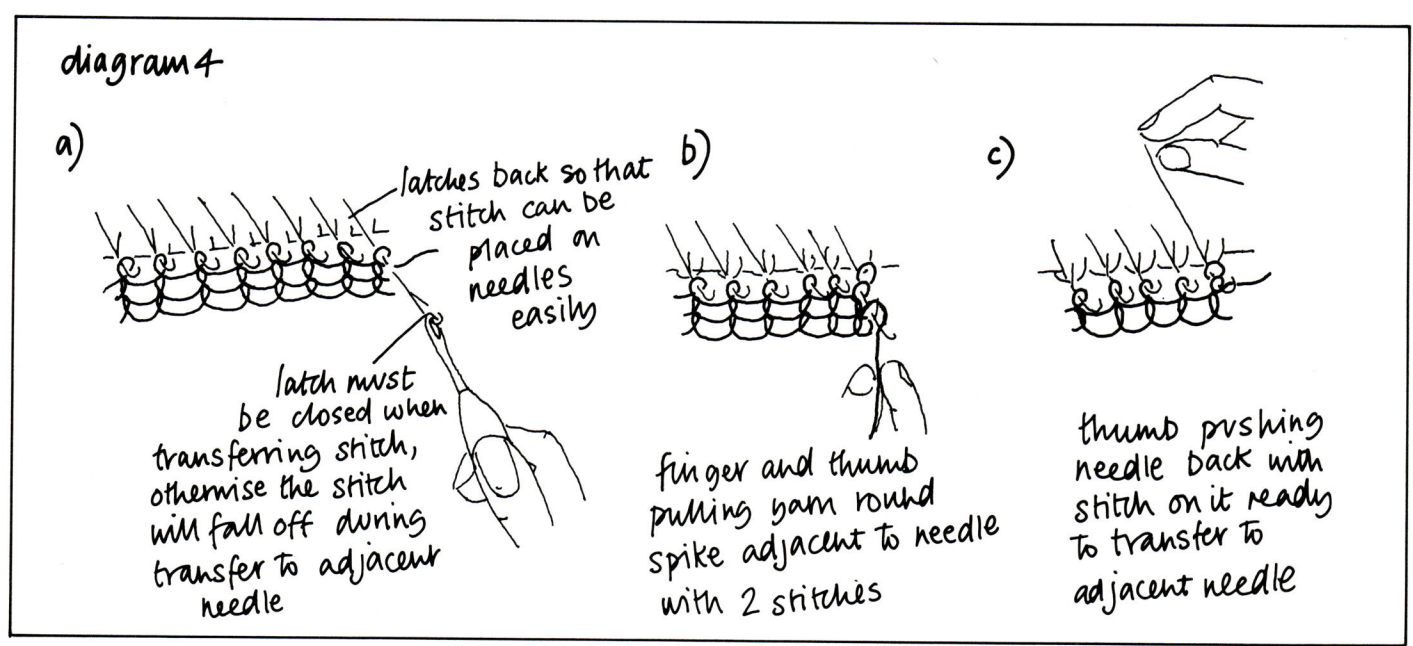

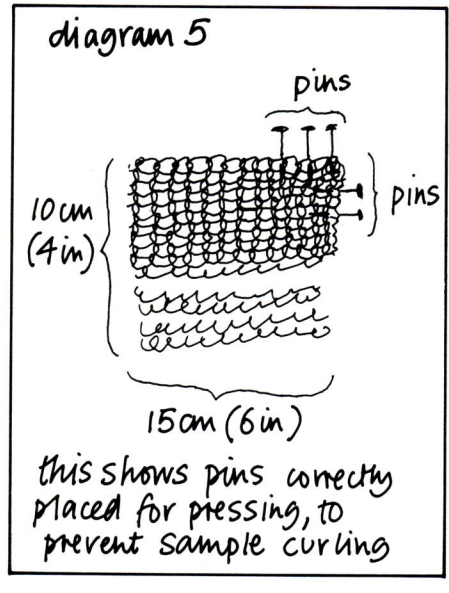

If not, adjust your tension dial accordingly and try again. Knit as many swatches as necessary to arrive at one that you feel will work for the bandeau. It is vital that you should be completely satisfied with all the qualities of the fabric you have just made before embarking on the project itself.

Diagram 6
Measuring yourself is the next step. Because knitting stretches, it is here advisable to subtract 5cm (2in) from your width measurement (but not from your length!). Depending on how tight you want your bandeau, subtract more or less from the width – this is entirely up to you. Having established the proportions of the garment you want, making sure that you have allowed enough depth to avoid the bandeau creeping up to expose more midriff than anticipated – unless, of course, you want to expose it – you are ready to count the number of stitches and rows per 2.5cm (1in) of your tension swatch.

Diagram 7
Lay the knitted sample square and flat and count the stitches over 10cm (4in) using a rigid ruler or tape measure. Estimate as closely as possible how many stitches there are to 2.5cm (1in). Then count the number of rows in the same way. Write the figures down in your notebook, together with your own measurements. Multiply the stitches per 2.5cm (1in) by the girth to give you the correct number of stitches to cast on. With this information, together with the number on the

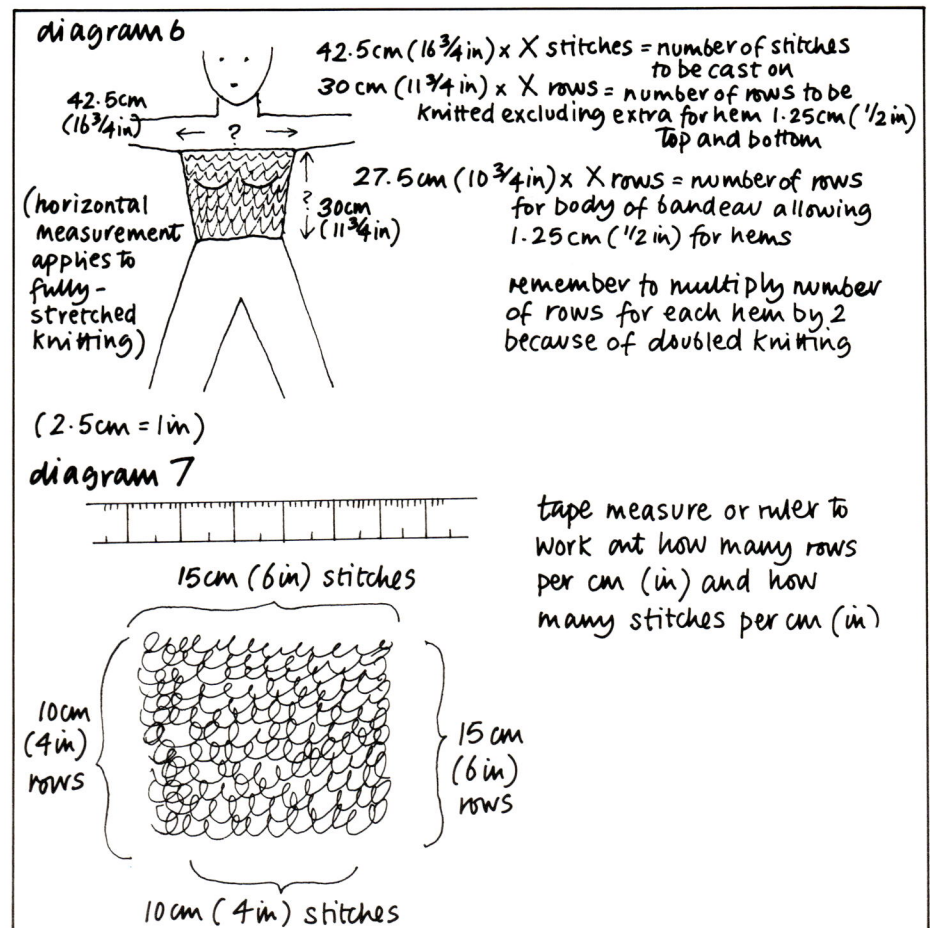

diagram 6

42.5cm (16¾in) x X stitches = number of stitches to be cast on
30cm (11¾in) x X rows = number of rows to be knitted excluding extra for hem 1.25cm (½in) Top and bottom

27.5cm (10¾in) x X rows = number of rows for body of bandeau allowing 1.25cm (½in) for hems

remember to multiply number of rows for each hem by 2 because of doubled knitting

42.5cm (16¾in)

(horizontal measurement applies to fully-stretched knitting)

30cm (11¾in)

(2.5cm = 1in)

diagram 7

15cm (6in) stitches

10cm (4in) rows

15cm (6in) rows

10cm (4in) stitches

tape measure or ruler to work out how many rows per cm (in) and how many stitches per cm (in)

another unhappy knitter with yarn threaded correctly but pulled too tight

ball of yarn should remain on table

tension dials probably too tight

tension dial you found most suitable, you are now ready to cast on the hem edge of the bandeau.

The garment will need a strong edge to prevent it curling, making a hem very necessary. This should be knitted on a tension set one number lower (tighter) than that of the main piece of knitting. As the hem will have to take the strain of most of your body movement it is likely to stretch more than the rest of the garment, so making it slightly tighter will help considerably.

The depth of your hem has to be taken into account when estimating the length of the bandeau and should be included in the total measurement.

Make it between 1.25cm (½in) and 2cm (¾in) in depth. It will be double thickness, so you will have a front and back and a fold-line along the bottom edge.

Using waste yarn similar in weight to your chosen yarn, cast on the required number of stitches. Position the weights, set your tension dial and knit several rows ending with the carriage on your left. Cut the waste yarn, remove it from the yarn break and the other end of the carriage. Thread a length of slippery yarn or fine nylon cord – about 1m (1yd) will do – through the carriage yarn feeder. Knit one row with this and then remove the left-over cord from the carriage.

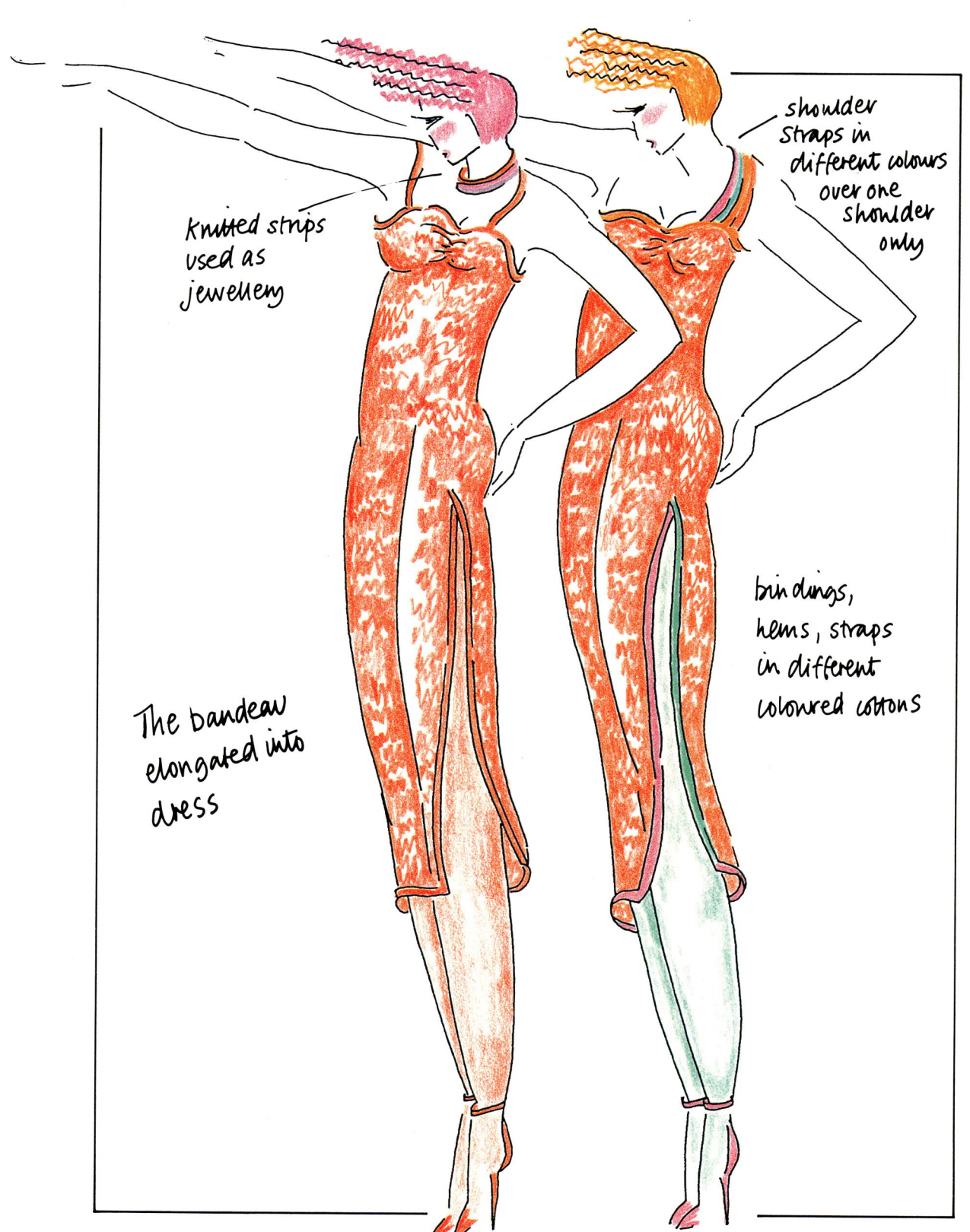

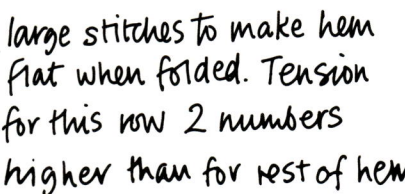

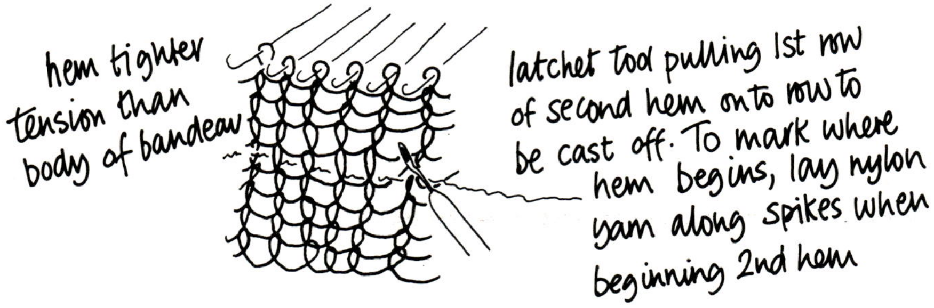

Diagram 8
You are now ready to begin the hem. Check that the tension is one number less than that required for the bandeau and knit as many rows as you require for the depth. Before knitting the back or inside of the hem, adjust the tension dial two numbers higher for the fold-line of the hem, knit one row (to create the fold-line) and then return it to its original position. Repeat the number of rows knitted for the front of the hem.

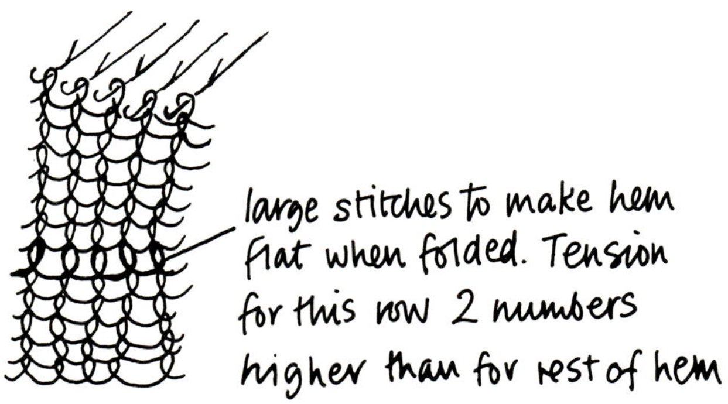

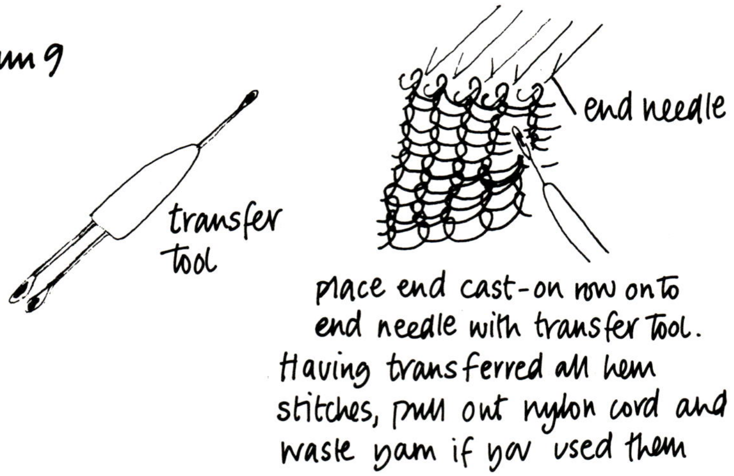

Diagram 9
You now have to pick up the stitches from the first row you knitted in the correct yarn for the bandeau. This is not as difficult as it sounds. All you have to do is place them, one by one, and using the transfer tool, over the stitches already occupying the needles. You will find this much easier if you begin at one end and work across rather than trying to start somewhere in the middle. Once this rather fiddly stage has been accomplished, all the needles should hold two stitches each. You can now change to a looser tension so that it is correct for the main part of the bandeau.

Diagram 10
Having knitted the depth of fabric required except for the measurement allowed for the top hem, you have to now repeat the operation with which you started, but in reverse. Remember to adjust the tension dial three times as before.

Diagram 11
Pick up all the stitches so that you have two on every needle as before, then cast off two by two. To ensure the edge is even and not too tight or loose, loop the yarn around the spike adjacent to the needle on which each pair is to be cast off. Do this in the same way as for the tension swatch, the only difference being that now you are casting off two stitches at a time instead of one.

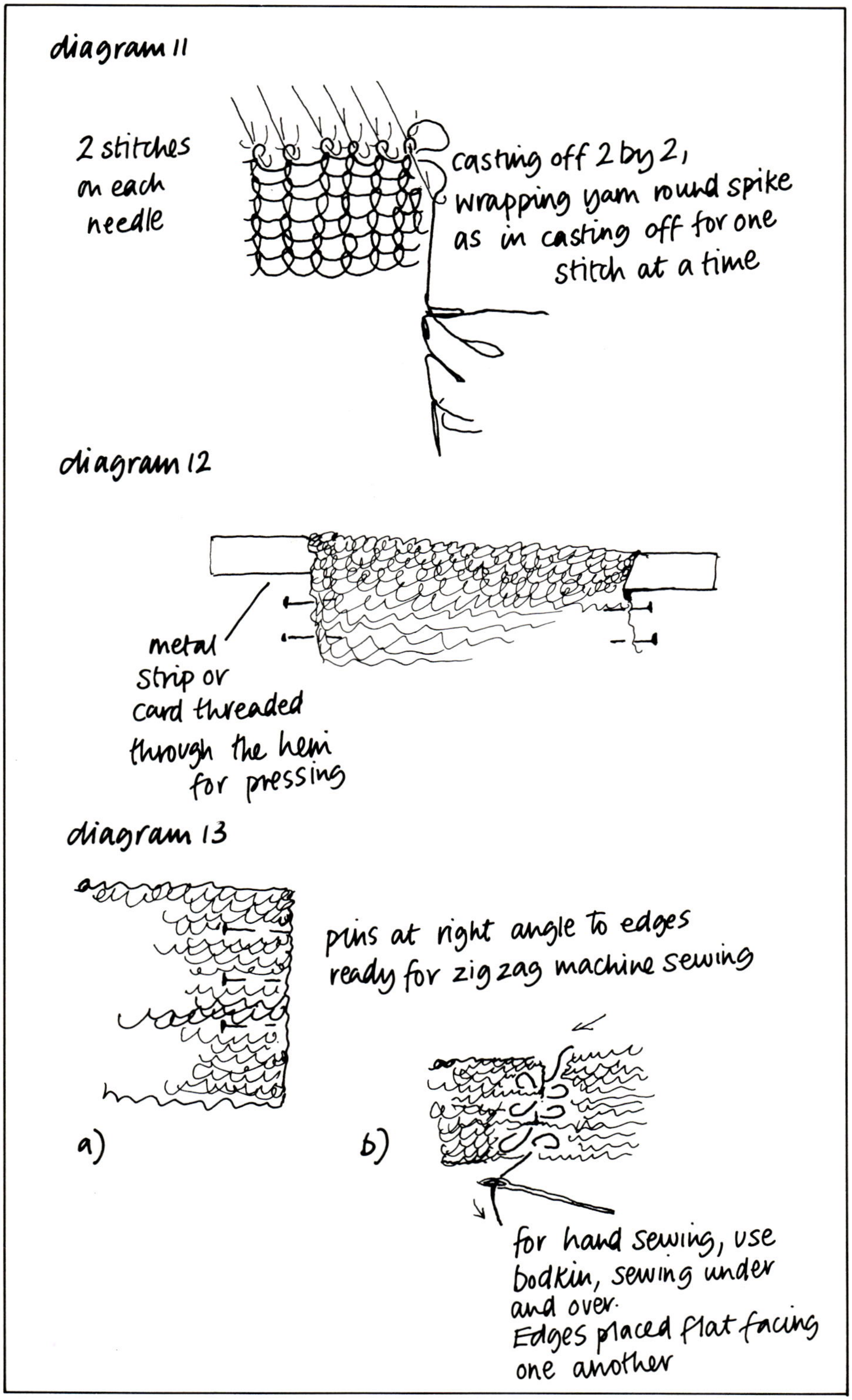

Diagram 12

You now have a strip of knitting with a hem at the top and bottom. Press it carefully in the same way as for the tension sample. In order to keep the hem even however, slot a thin length of card or a rustproof metal strip through each hem as it is pressed. Pull it out when the hem is dry.

Diagram 13

Pin the shorter edges of the bandeau, inserting the pins at right angles (a). Then, if you have a sewing machine, zigzag stitch together; if not, sew it by hand. If the latter, place the edges so that they face each other and use a bodkin threaded with the same yarn as the bandeau to link them together (b). Sew it row by row, catching the outside stitch each time. This ensures that the seam lies flat.

diagram 11

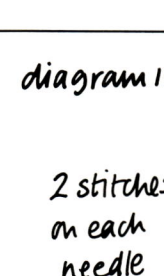
2 stitches on each needle

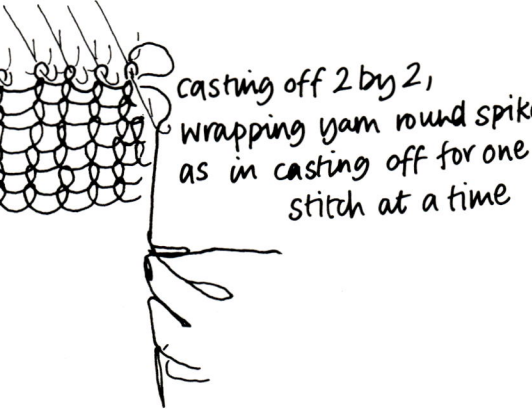
casting off 2 by 2, wrapping yarn round spike as in casting off for one stitch at a time

diagram 12

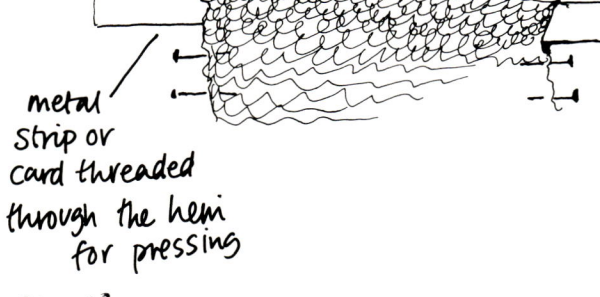
metal strip or card threaded through the hem for pressing

diagram 13

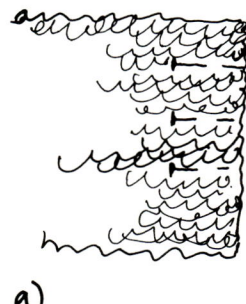
a)

pins at right angle to edges ready for zig zag machine sewing

b)

for hand sewing, use bodkin, sewing under and over. Edges placed flat facing one another

YES IT FITS PERFECTLY! WELL DONE

And that is that. Your first bandeau is finished and you can put it on. It should fit! If it does not, it is back to the knitting machine, I am afraid. Assuming it does, it is time to knit another one.

Choose another yarn, knit a tension swatch to find the correct tension, then make another bandeau, in exactly the same way: it should take you half the time of the first. This time, however, you are not going to sew it up, but fasten the garment with ties or knitted rouleaux – made on your machine. Because you are working on a single bed machine, the edges of knitting tend to curl – you will have noticed this when making up tension swatches – and knitting rouleaux is a way of utilizing this tendency.

Diagram 14

If you cast on about six stitches and knit between 10 and 20 rows, once the piece has been removed from the machine you will see that in section it appears almost round. A strip knitted in this way is called – or I call it – a rouleau. Use them to tie the front opening of this bandeau.

Before knitting any rouleaux, decide how many you need. This will very much depend on how much bust you have or do not have, and how much exposure you want. I suggest you make four to six pairs of rouleaux and see how you get on. Decide how long you want them to be – between 20cm (8in) and 25cm (10in) should be adequate – and then note this down.

Diagram 15

Cast on for the rouleaux in the same way you would for a tension swatch. Knit the second row and again push out the needles, deciding whether to add weights or, if the knitting is progressing smoothly enough, not. Use the same tension as for the hems of the bandeau and, when the length of the rouleau has been knitted, cast off. Write down the number of rows shown on the counter so that all the following rouleaux will be the same length. If you feel slightly – or very, as the case may be – insecure in your bandeau, consider using rouleaux for shoulder straps. If you do not feel like having them all in one colour, knit them in other colours, but do remember to use the same yarn and the same tension, otherwise you have to go back to square one knitting another series of tension swatches.

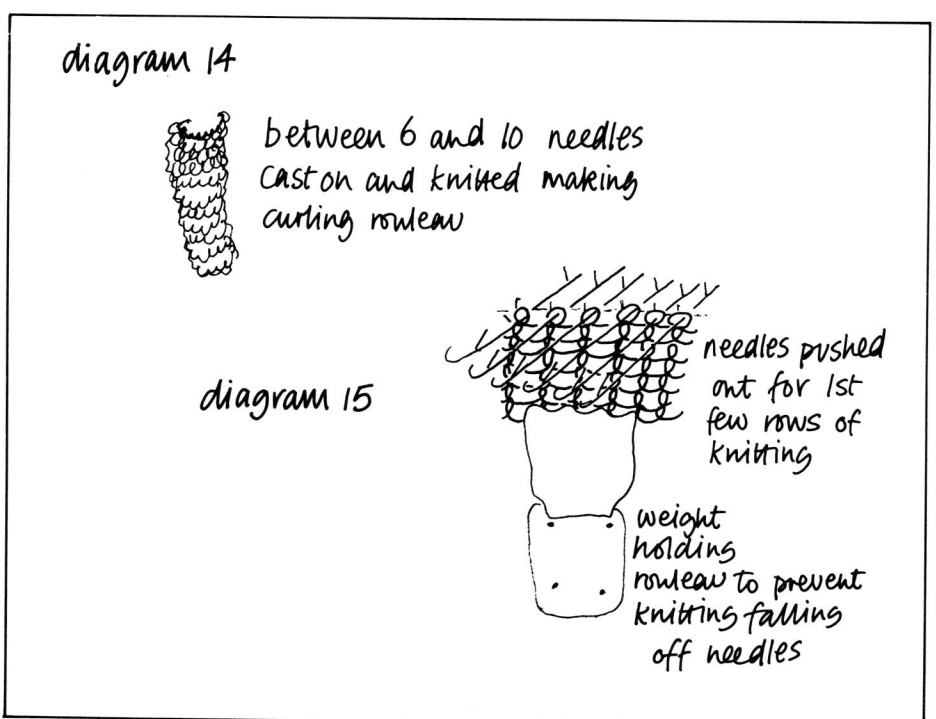

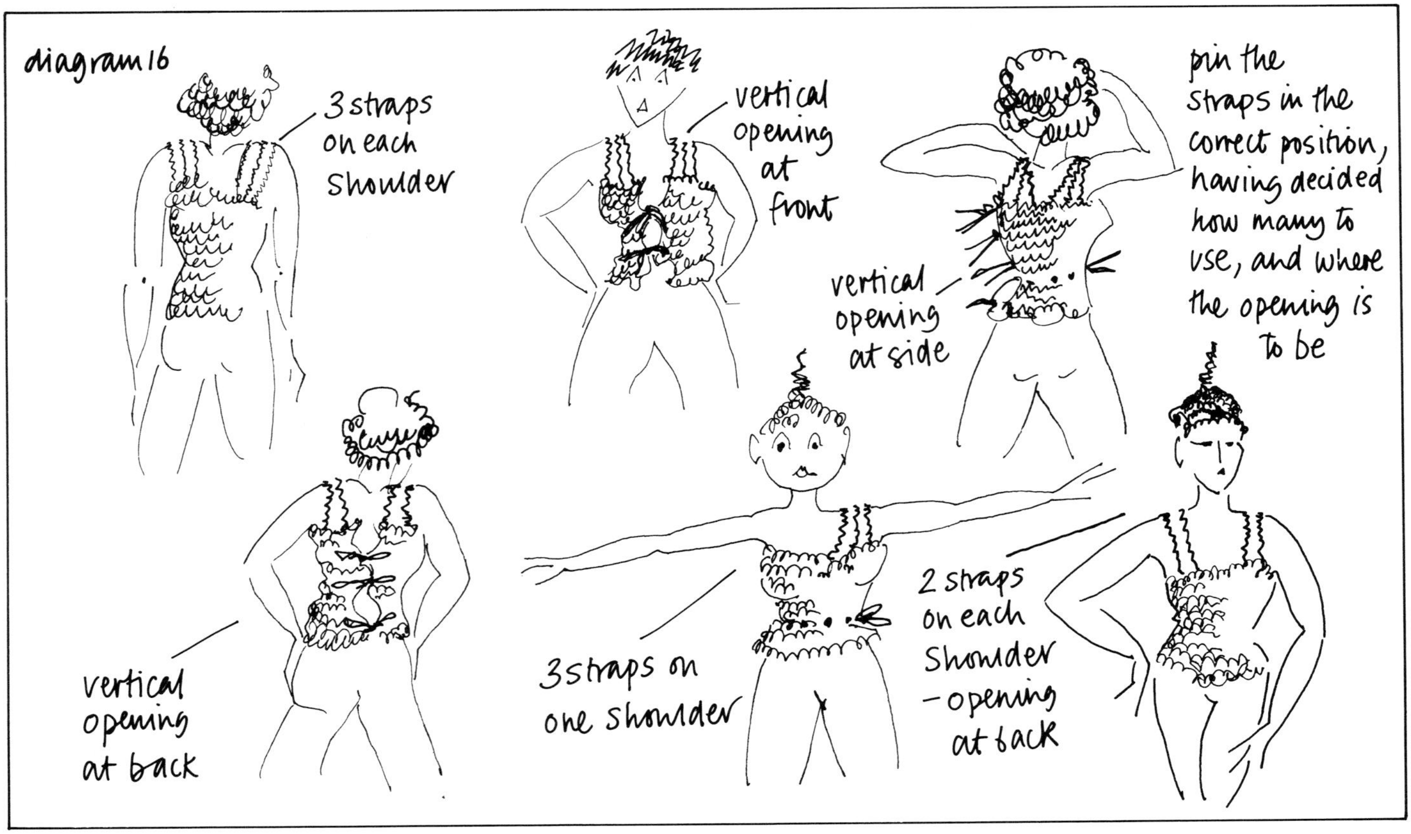

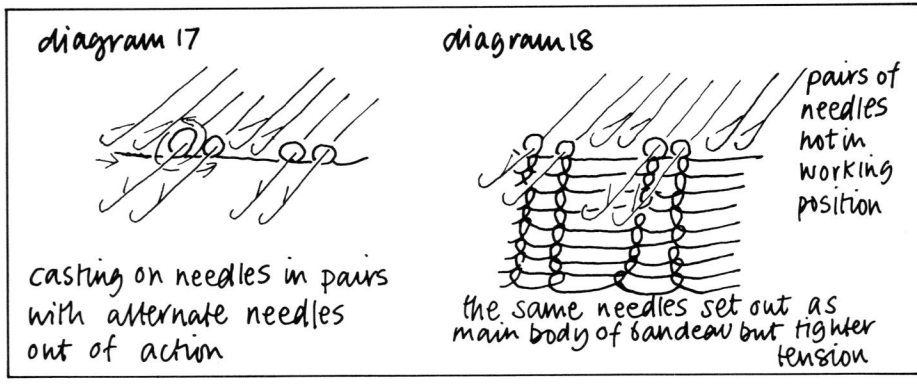

To estimate the length of shoulder straps, put on your bandeau and then measure the distance between the point of attachment on the back and that on the front. Crossover straps will be longer. If you want several straps, knit the required number.

Diagram 16

Before pinning them into place, decide where you want the vertical opening to be. Once the decision is made, pin the rouleaux or straps in place and sew them on with fine cotton matching the colour of the bandeau.
Your second bandeau is now complete. Change into it and then step back from the mirror to admire your progress – and yourself!

Diagram 17

With two excellent knitted bandeaux to your credit, it is time to try another technique. Instead of casting on to every one needle, try casting on each second pair of needles – on two, off two, on two and so on. Make sure as you do so that all the pairs of needles not required for knitting are pushed out of the working position. Cast on in this manner until you have 20 needles in action.

Knit a tension swatch on these 20 needles, then write down the number of rows and stitches per 2.5cm (1in).

Diagram 18

If this swatch proves satisfactory, cast on the required number of stitches for the hem, making sure to alter your tension as with the first two bandeaux.

Knit the main body of the garment together with its hem and then cast off. Press in the usual manner.

Diagram 19

It may be that you fancy lacing up the front of this third design rather than sewing the short sides together. If so, you will want hems not only on the top and bottom edges, but the sides as well. The simplest way to do this is to bind the front edges with rouleaux. Knit two to the correct length, press them flat (a) and then place the outside edge of the bandeau to one long outer edge of one rouleau, right sides together. Pin at right angles to the edge (b). Machine stitch in place with a slight zigzag or overlock or sew a back seam by hand. Turn the rouleau to the inside of the bandeau (c) so that the edge is bound and hem-stitch the other edge into place. Repeat on the other front edge.

Diagram 20

If a flatter edge is preferred (like the hems), hook the side stitches (those at the end of each row) on to your machine, making sure you do this with the inside – or wrong side – of the bandeau towards you. Knit a hem and cast off. Repeat on the other edge and then press as for the top and bottom edges.

Diagram 21

The trellis structure of the fabric you have just created for your third bandeau lends itself to threading for three dimensional surface decoration. Knit a long rouleau using the same technique as for the ties and thread through the pressed fabric at regular or irregular intervals, just as you like. You can sew in the ends on the wrong side or tie in a half bow. If you feel that a rouleau knitted in the same yarn may make the garment too bulky, consider using ribbons or rouleaux knitted in a lighter yarn with, perhaps, a silky quality. There are a whole host of alternatives.

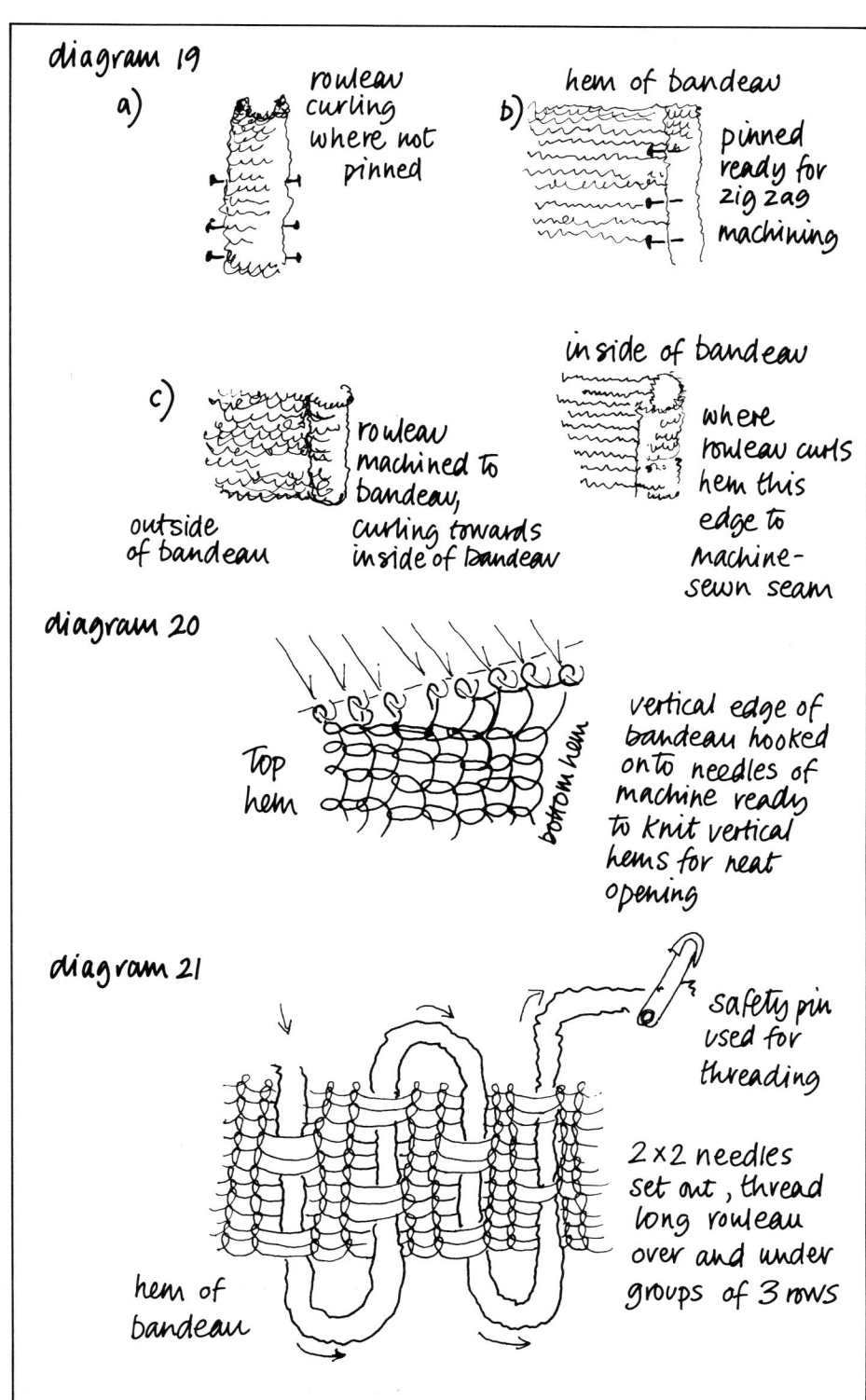

19

You are now the owner of three bandeaux and already have a fair grasp of how to use a single bed machine. Before progressing to further experimentation, try the same principles on a double bed machine for an understanding of the essential differences between the two types of knitting machine. A diagram will best describe these.

Diagram 22

As you will already have learned from the introduction at the beginning of the book, a single bed machine has one bed of needles, a double bed two. The single bed will knit single knitting and single knitting only. A double bed can knit single and double knitting. A second advantage of the double bed is that because it is able to knit two layers of knitting, it can be used to knit tubes, vertically and horizontally. To make a tension swatch using a double bed machine, start by making sure that the racking handle is down. Check that you have 20 needles in the knitting position on both beds and then cast on with waste yarn.

— deservedly proud knitter wearing bandeau

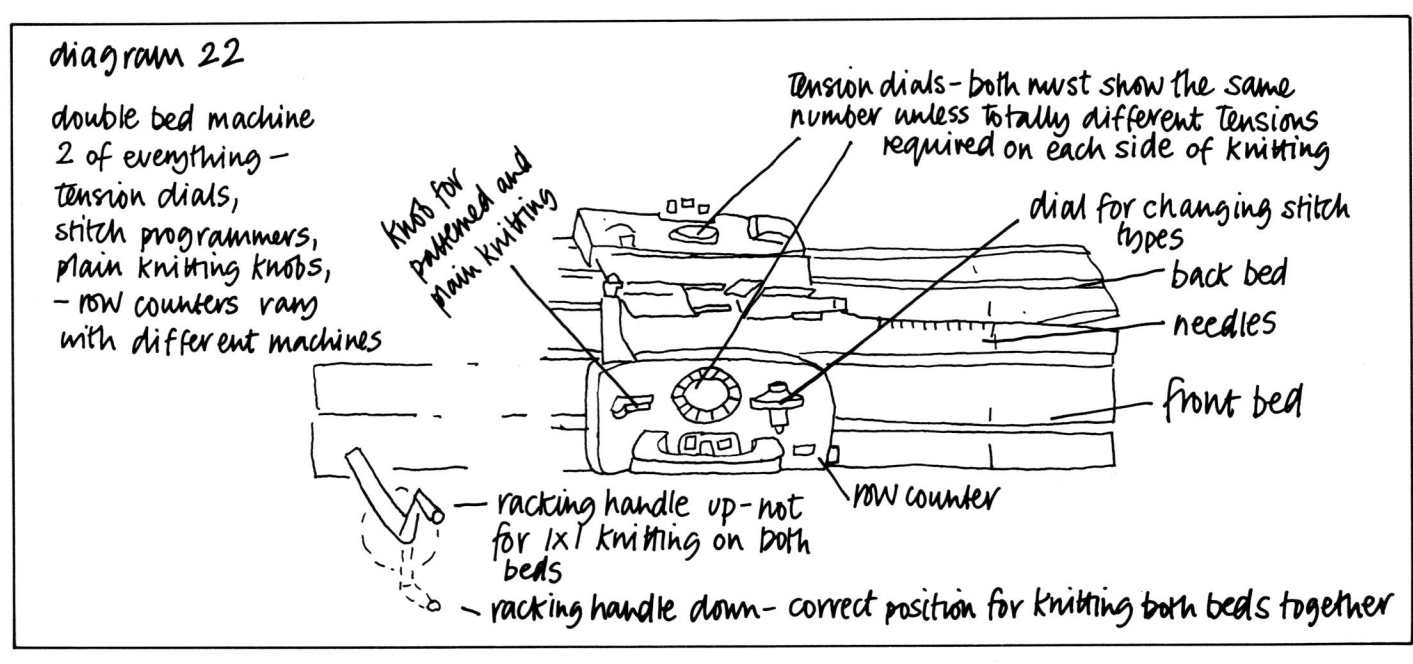

diagram 22

double bed machine 2 of everything — tension dials, stitch programmers, plain knitting knobs, — row counters vary with different machines

Knob for patterned and plain knitting

Tension dials - both must show the same number unless totally different tensions required on each side of knitting

dial for changing stitch types
back bed
needles
front bed
row counter

— racking handle up - not for 1x1 knitting on both beds

— racking handle down - correct position for knitting both beds together

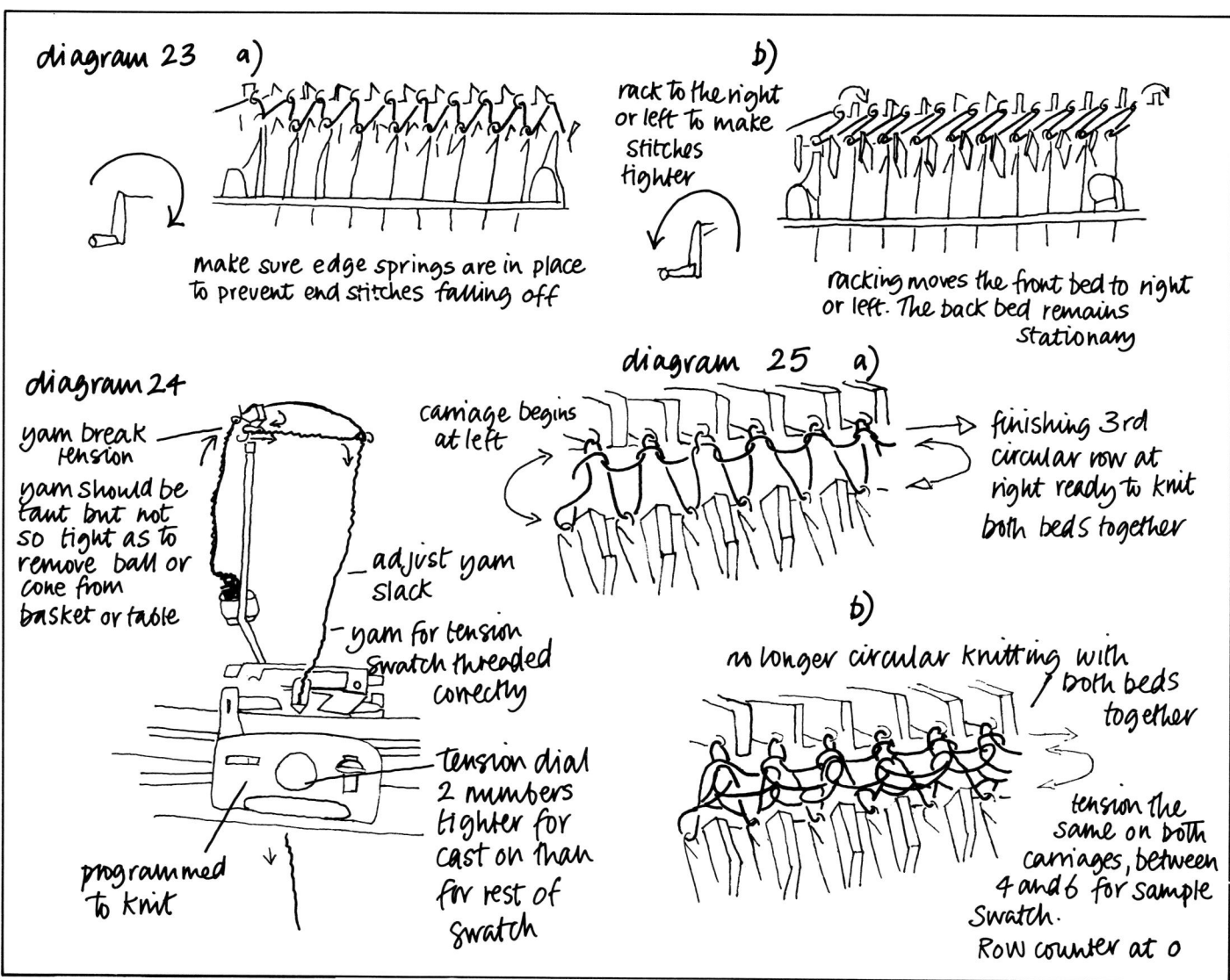

Diagram 23
Having cast on (a), rack one revolution to the right, knit a row then rack one revolution to the left (b). Continue knitting several rows without racking. Prepare for casting on your main yarn. Put the front carriage on to 'free move' so that it will not knit. Using the back bed only, knit four rows. Remove the yarn from the yarn feed and then knit two rows without yarn. This will result in the stitches coming off the back bed, but not the front.

Diagram 24
Thread the yarn to be used for the main part of the bandeau through the feed. Adjust the tension dial to a higher number than actually required for the garment itself, and then adjust the carriage so that both beds are programmed to knit.

Diagram 25
Knit one row and then programme the machine to knit one bed at a time (refer back to diagram 22 to see how it produces tubular or circular knitting). Knit three rows, one on the front and two on the back. The carriage should now be on the right-hand side (a). Re-programme the machine to knit both beds at the same time (b). Knit two rows. Change the tension so that it is between two and six, then move the row counter to zero so that you can count the number of rows for the tension swatch.

Diagram 26
With the square complete you must cast off. This requires all the stitches being transferred from the front bed to the back; you can either do this one stitch at a time or use what is called a multiple transfer tool. Casting off on to a double bed is very similar to doing so on a single bed except that sometimes you do not have any spikes to loop the yarn around. To maintain an even edge, it sometimes helps to loop some of the cast-off stitches on to the emptied needles.

Diagram 27
Study your tension sample and imagine it made up into a bandeau. But perhaps you can visualize it as a long tube dress – an elongated bandeau with a slit or slits at the side. It will obviously take longer to make but with a knitting machine it should not take too long. Write down your measurements and work out how many stitches and rows you will need, allowing for the hems in the usual way (diagrams 8 and 9). Having cast on the appropriate number of stitches for the first side with waste yarn, – you are going to knit a front and back separately – prepare to transfer to the main yarn. Check that both edge springs – if your machine has them – are in position. Make sure that the tension is two numbers higher than that used for the tension sample and that your row counter is set to zero.

Diagram 28
Knit the number of rows you need for the tubular hem, making a note of the number just knitted so that you can repeat them exactly for the other side. Turn the row counter back to zero again. Knit the number of rows required for the dress, then, referring back to your notebook, knit the top hem in the same way as for the bottom. Make a note of the rows knitted for the body of the garment. Cast off.
Knit another piece exactly the same. Press both, making sure that you do

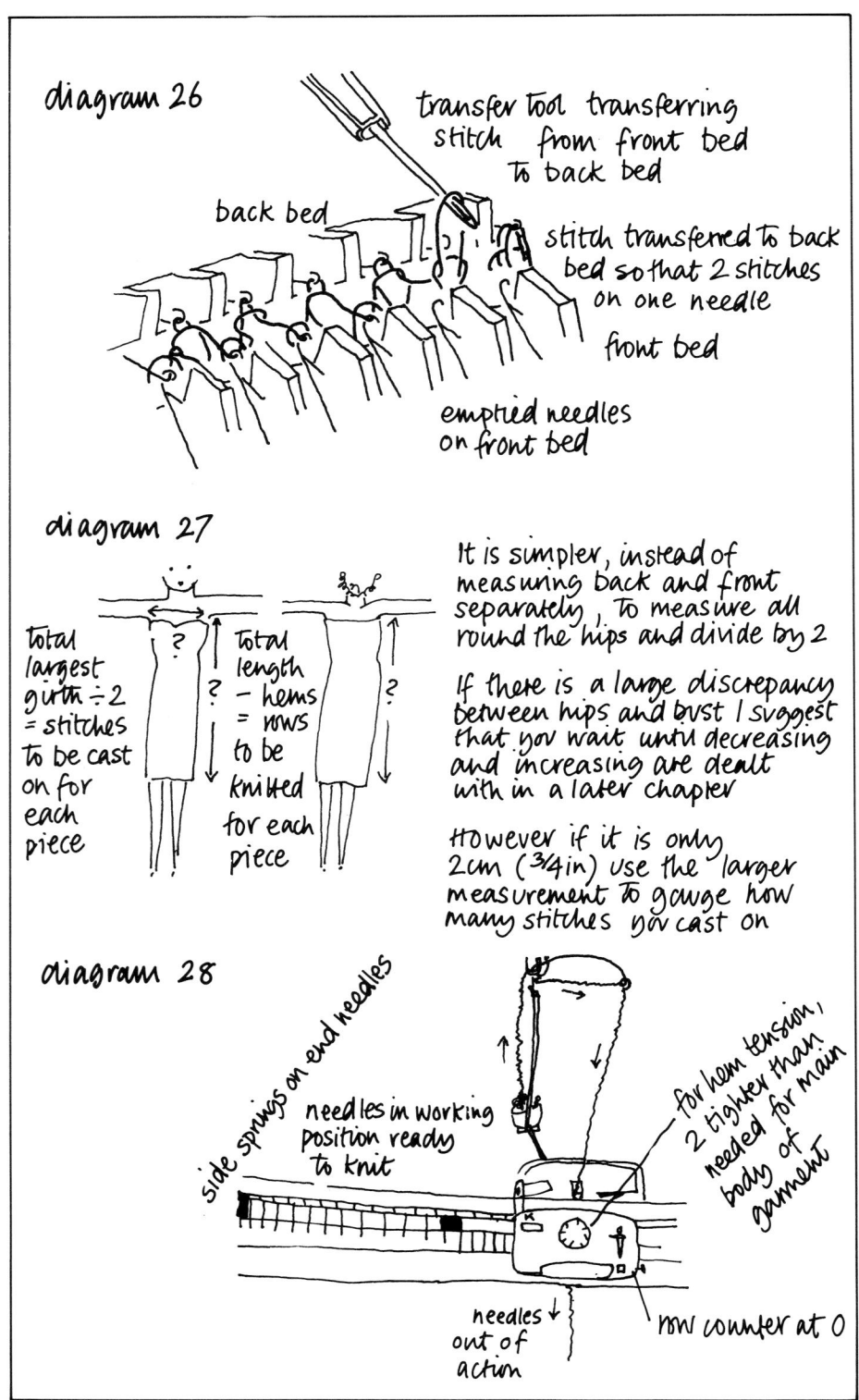

not stretch one any more than the other. You should now have two quite symmetrical rectangles ready for assembly. If you want to bind the slit or slits at the hem, decide on their length and write this down. Also work out the width of the required bindings.

Diagram 29
For shoulder straps and slit bindings you need flat lengths of knitted fabric rather than rouleaux, though this is, of course, entirely up to you. If you do decide to follow the course I suggest, use the fabric created for the hem as your tension swatch.
Cast on as many stitches as you need, knit for the length required and then cast off. Return the counter to zero and repeat for another strip. Press.

Diagram 30
Establish where you want them to be attached to the dress and mark with pins. Assemble the dress as described for the bandeau (diagram 13), using a machine or sewing by hand (a). Bind the slit edges by hand with the strips of knitting, overlapping at the top (b), then press neatly.

Diagram 31
Leave the front of the dress plain, or ruche by stitching twice between the bust (a). Either use shirring elastic wound on to the bobbin for stretch, or large stitches pulled to gather the fabric. Sew in any stray ends by hand on the wrong side (b). If you want straps, knit strips similar to those you made for the bindings and attach them so that they go over the shoulders or make one to go diagonally from the front across the opposite shoulder and down the back.
Try on your new dress and congratulate yourself for having learned so much in one day. Everything should fit beautifully and with Monday's crash programme completed, you deserve to enjoy your new wardrobe. Relax now; tomorrow is another day, with even more to do.

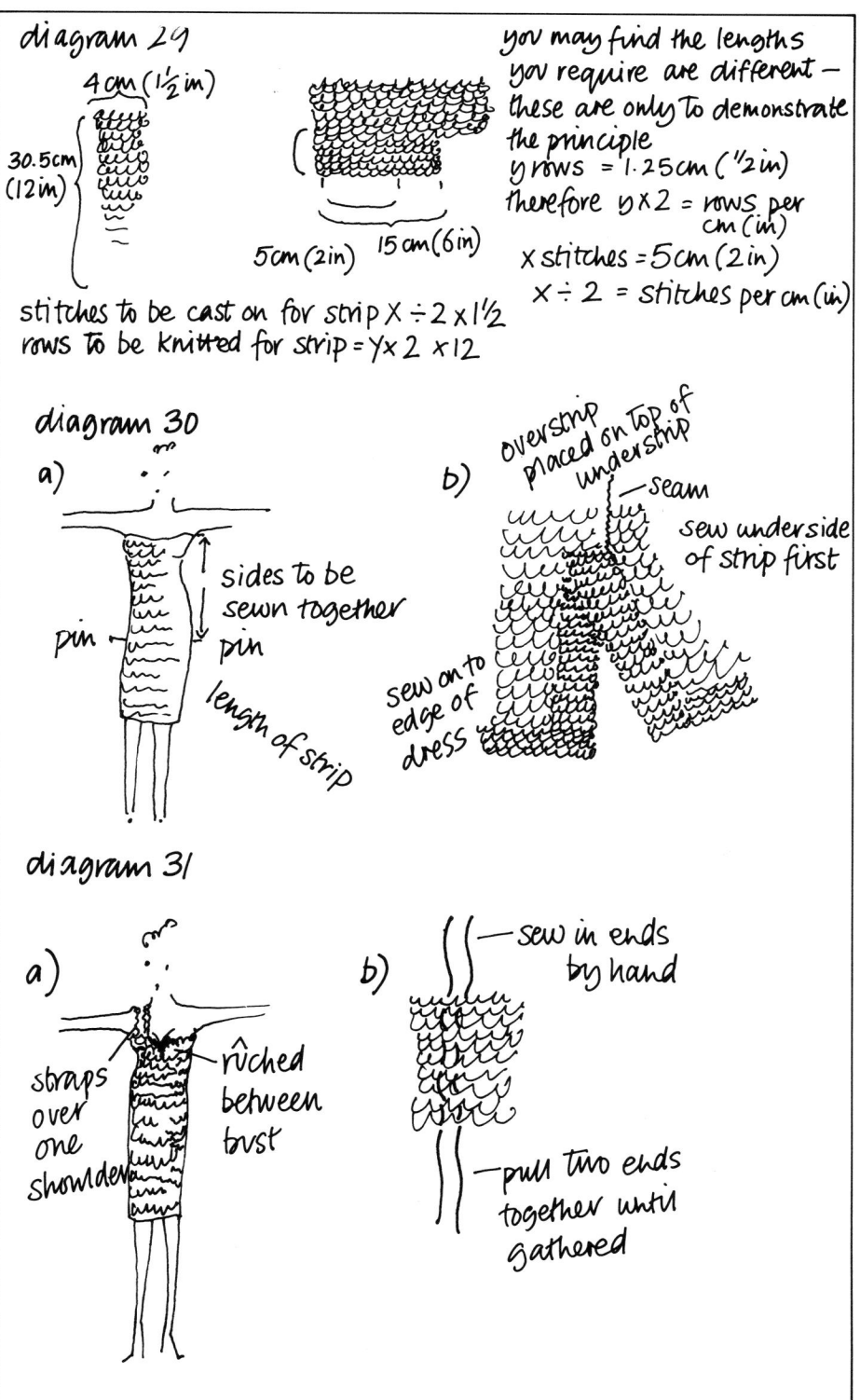

Tuesday

The techniques tackled on Monday were aimed to inspire confidence. They succeeded. Today, Tuesday, you have no need to flaunt this new found assurance; and after such obvious exuberance you want a complete contrast: restraint and understatement. This is exactly what is proposed.

Having read the newspaper and your letters, drunk coffee, eaten toast and marmalade and executed all those other essential breakfast tasks, you are ready to concentrate on Tuesday's project. You will learn how to knit a simple sweater, using many of the techniques remembered from Monday together with enough new ones to encourage you to feel that you are making further progress.

As I said, Tuesday is to be a more subtle day than Monday, so the garment you will be knitting should suit this more restrained mood. First, collect as many yarns in neutral tones of varying thicknesses, weight, fibre content and texture that you have to hand. Select six. This should be enough to start with.

First swatch using thick and thin yarn

Sample swatch for sweater with side edge cast on for hem

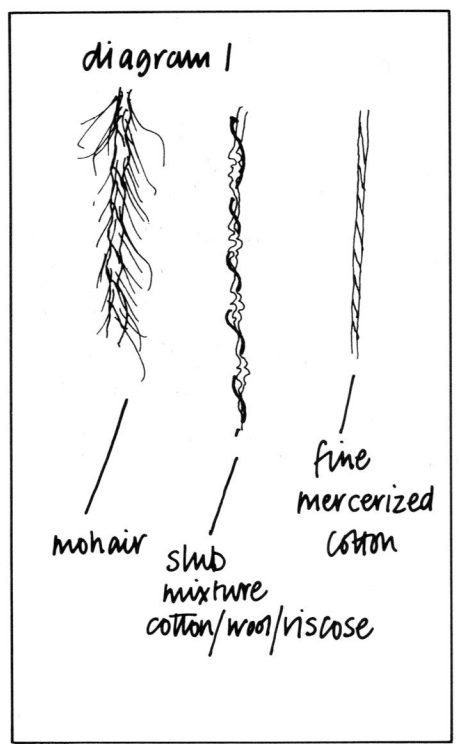

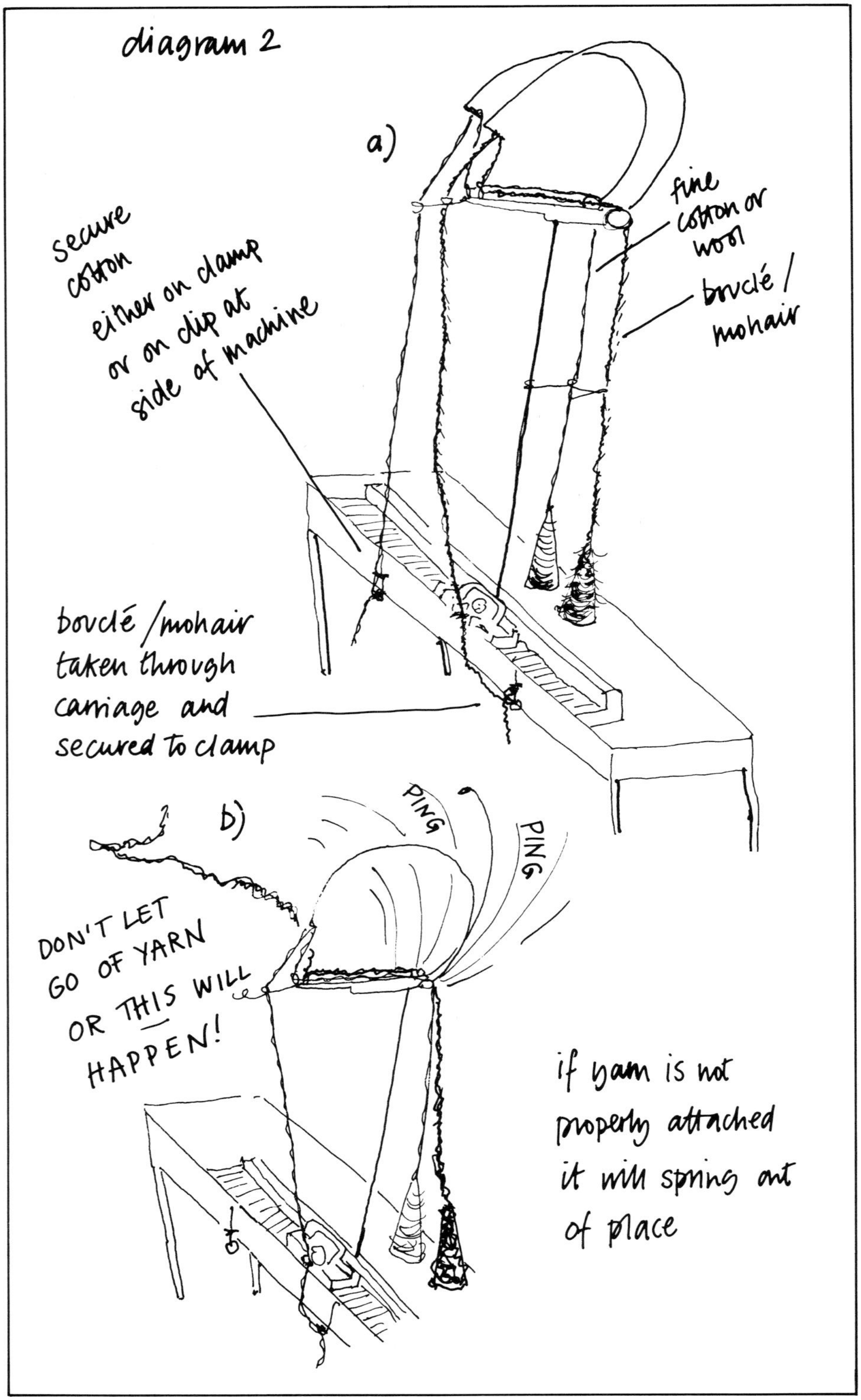

Diagram 1
Thread your machine with two yarns: one thick, one thin. If you need reminding how to thread it correctly, refer back to Monday's diagrams. The two yarns should contrast as much as possible – a fine wool or mercerized cotton similar in weight to that used on Monday (only in a beige or cream) and a slub, twisted wool, viscose and cotton mixture or, perhaps, a mohair.

Diagram 2
Having threaded the thick yarn as you did for Monday's project, thread the finer through the spare feed. However, instead of pulling it through the carriage feed, attach it to the side or to one of the machine clamps so that it is secured well out of the way (a). Check that your machine looks as in the first diagram rather than the second (b) which shows what would happen if you let go of the yarn when it was not secured properly!

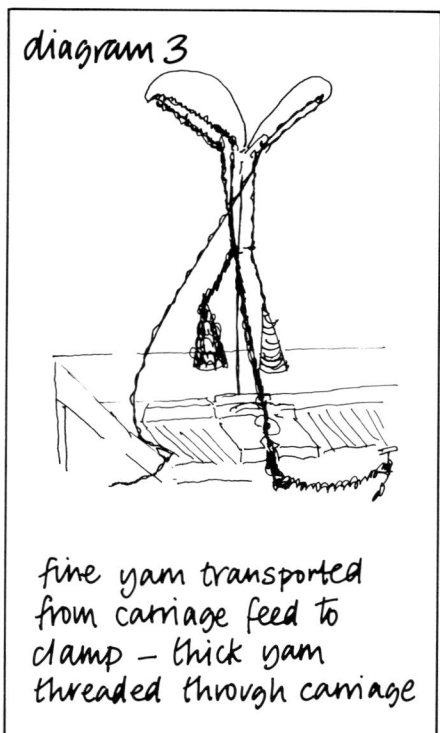

fine yarn transported from carriage feed to clamp – thick yarn threaded through carriage

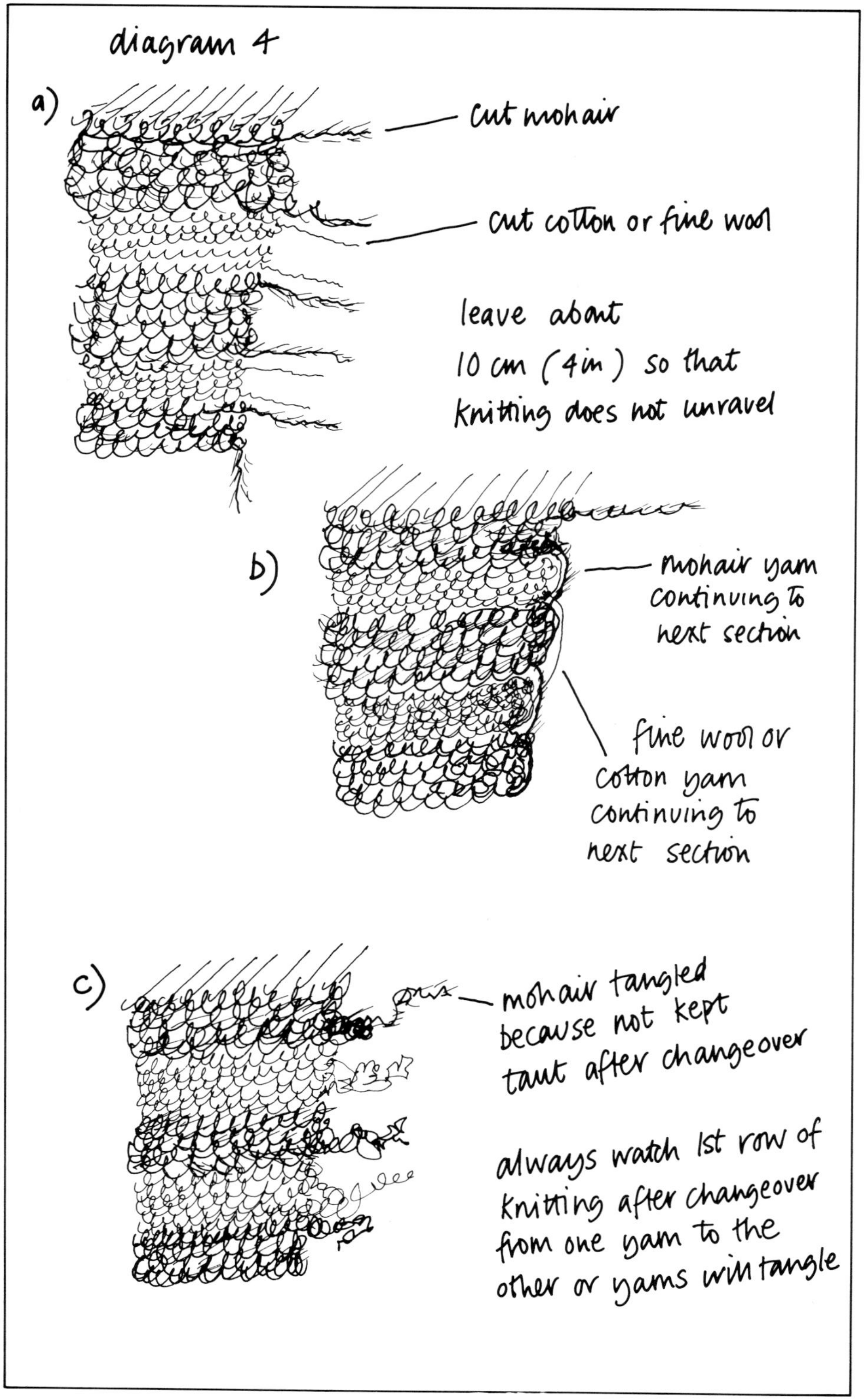

Diagram 3

Having fastened the thinner yarn out of the way correctly, you are now ready to make the first tension swatch of the day. Set the tension dial to eight and cast on with the thicker of the two yarns. Knit 10 rows; then alter the dial to three. Remove the thick yarn and tie it on to a clamp.

Diagram 4

Place the thinner yarn through the carriage feed and knit 10 rows at tension three. After these 10 rows, either cut the yarn, leaving a long end to tie on the thicker yarn and pull it through (a), or remove it from the carriage and replace with the thicker yarn. Make sure the yarn not in use is weighted down and well out of the way (b). Since this is your first swatch using several yarns, I suggest you cut each yarn at each changeover, leaving long enough ends so that your knitting does not unravel (c). Check at this stage that you are doing this.

diagram 4

a) cut mohair — cut cotton or fine wool — leave about 10 cm (4 in) so that knitting does not unravel

b) mohair yarn continuing to next section — fine wool or cotton yarn continuing to next section

c) mohair tangled because not kept taut after changeover

always watch 1st row of knitting after changeover from one yarn to the other or yarns will tangle

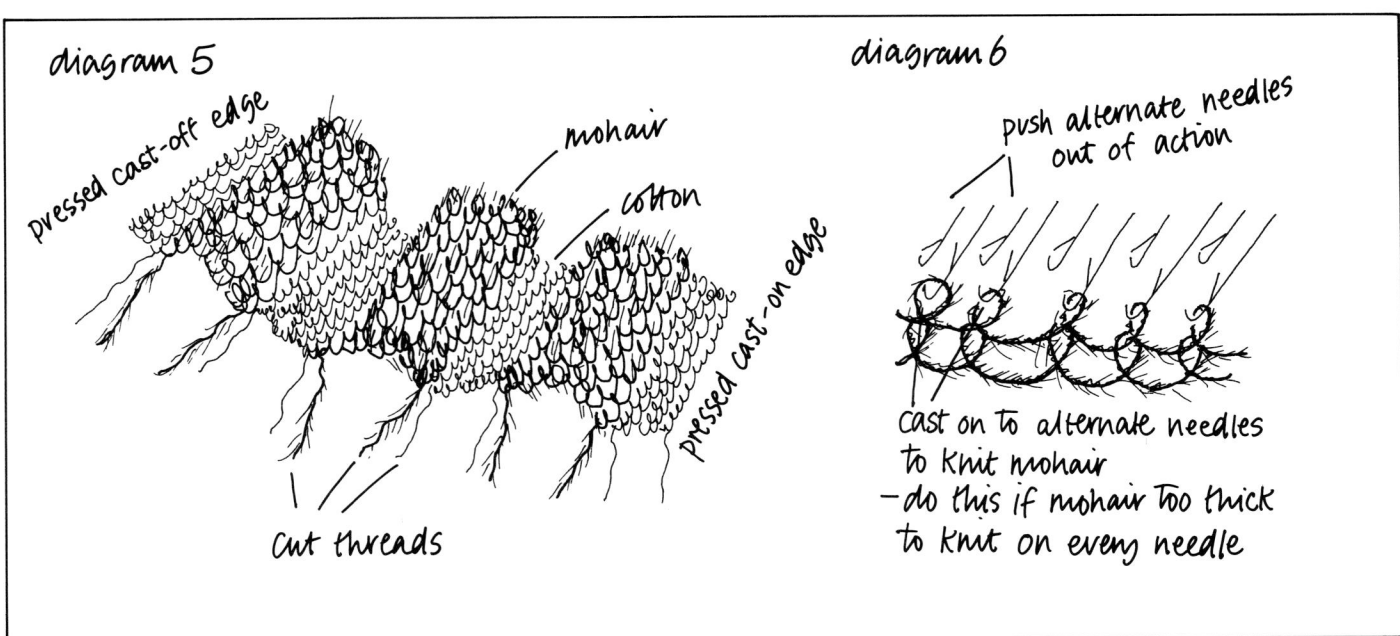

Diagram 5
After completing 80 rows, and having changed the yarn every 10 rows, cast off as you remember from chapter 1, diagram 4, referring back if necessary. This time, however, only press the cast-on and cast-off edges to prevent them curling. Now look at your completed swatch. Does it look right? The ridged effect gained from using two contrasting yarns will have been spoiled if you have pressed it all over, so let us hope it is not a tangled, flattened mess! For the moment, do not worry about the cut threads hanging from the sides of the swatch; we will attend to them later.

Diagram 6
Before moving on to creating your next swatch, make sure you like the first one. Is the tension for both yarns right? Is one too tight, or the other too loose, or vice versa? If the fabric you have knitted feels like corrugated cardboard, it is hardly the ideal fabric to wear next to your skin – or, for that matter, wear at all!
If the fabric is too hard, the thicker yarn you used was probably too bulky for your machine. If you knitted it up to a tension of 10, and the dial goes no higher, you may have to try casting it on to alternate needles for looser stitches or try another yarn altogether. Creating a fabric in this way is very much a matter of continual experimentation, trial and error and learning by your mistakes. What have you learned this time? That if your thicker yarn is not suitable, you can put away any yarns that are similar; trying them in this instance will be an obvious waste of time.
Repeat the swatch with different yarns if the first was not successful. They did work the first time round? Good. Now you can try another idea.

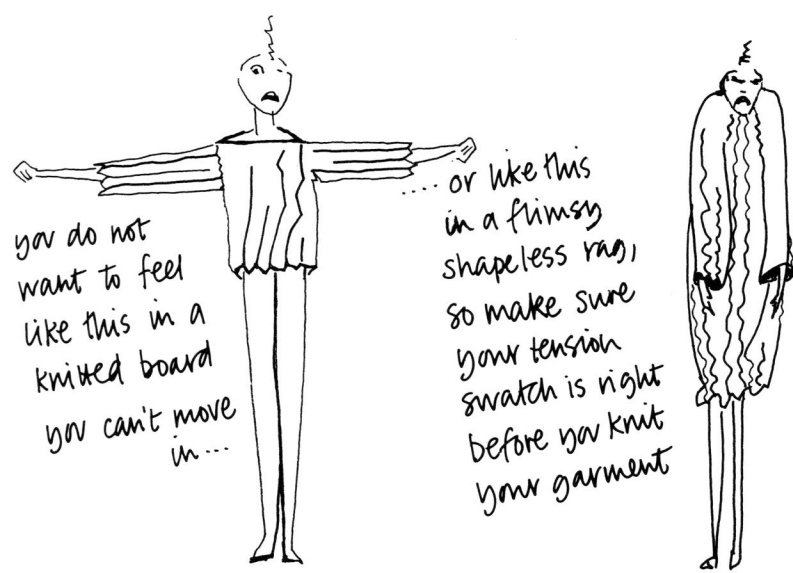

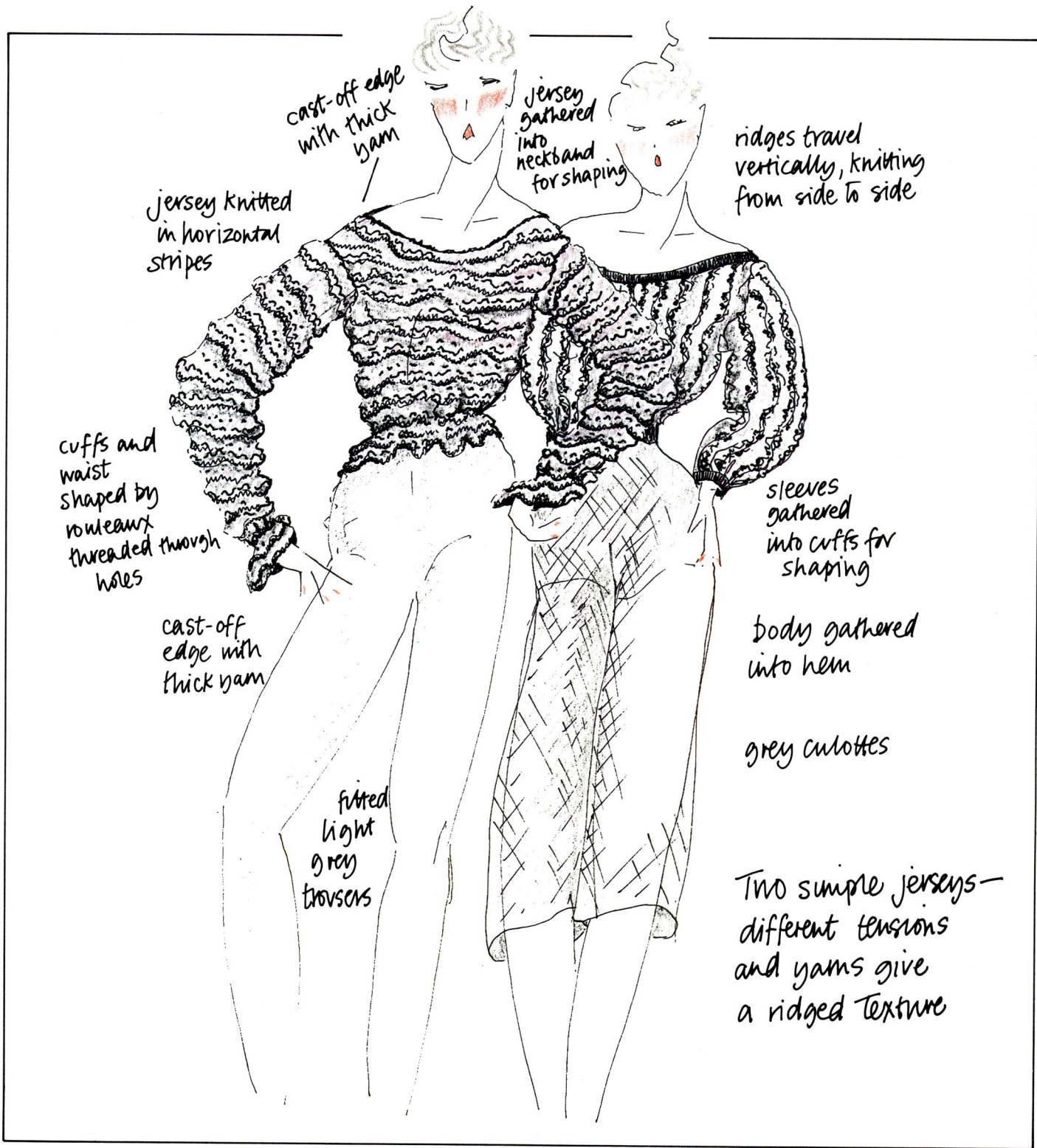

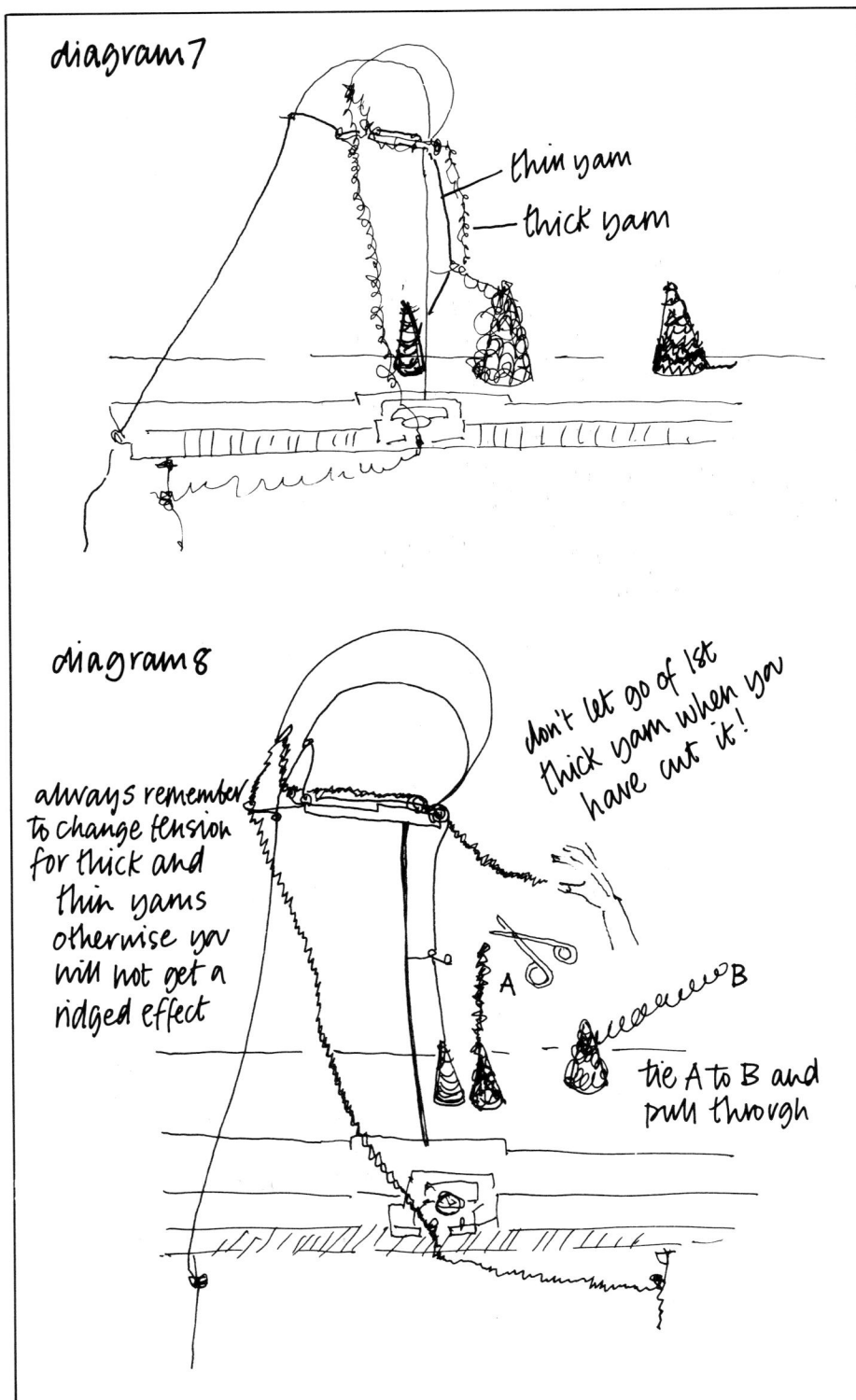

Choose three contrasting yarns: one thin and two thick. Thread the thinner yarn through one feeder and any one of the two others through the other feeder. Keep the third yarn beside the thicker yarn you have threaded up, but do not allow them to be so close that they inadvertently get tangled up.

Diagram 7
Begin as for the first swatch. Cast on with one of the thick yarns, knit 10 rows and then change to the thinner one and knit another 10 rows. Do not forget to alter your tension dial each time you change the yarn. Whereas in the first sample you would have changed to the first thicker yarn again, you must now change to the third yarn. Cut the original thicker yarn you have already used close to the cone and tie on the new yarn. Pull it through the carriage and now knit 10 rows. Always remember to change the tension each time you change from a thick to thin yarn and a thin to thick, otherwise you will not achieve the ridged effect you are after.

Diagram 8
Knit 10 rows using thin yarn, 10 rows using the third yarn, 10 rows using thin and then change back to the second yarn just as you did when introducing the third yarn into the swatch.

Diagram 9
Continue in this way until the sample is large enough to be cast off. Press in the same way as you did for the first tension sample, checking that the pattern is correct.

Diagram 10
Of course, you could cut and change your thick yarn for another thick yarn after every 10 rows of thin. In this instance, the ridges of thick yarn would be 20 rows deep instead of 10 rows deep. Even with the limitation of three yarns, there are several permutations to play around with. Try them.

diagram 9

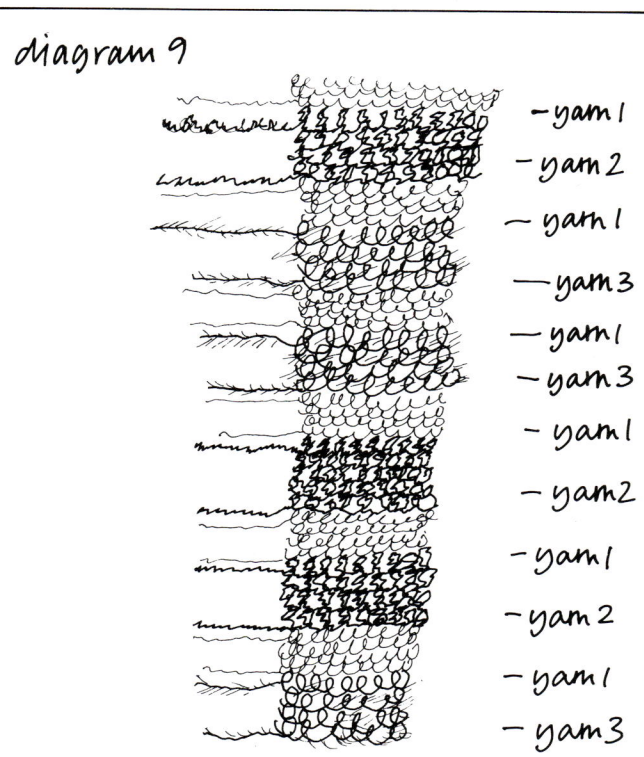

– yarn 1
– yarn 2
– yarn 1
– yarn 3
– yarn 1
– yarn 3
– yarn 1
– yarn 2
– yarn 1
– yarn 2
– yarn 1
– yarn 3

diagram 10

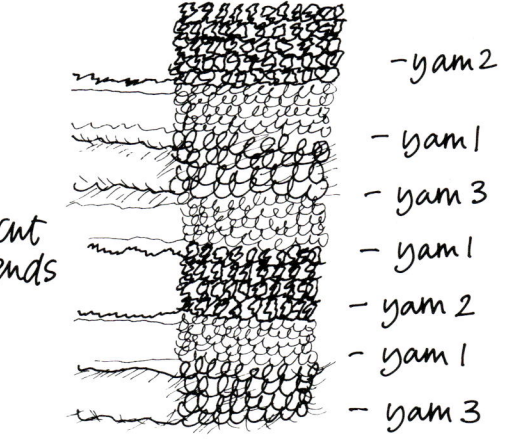

– yarn 2
– yarn 1
– yarn 3
– yarn 1
– yarn 2
– yarn 1
– yarn 3

cut ends

Three different yarns used for ridged effect

Three different grey yarns used for ridged effect

don't use too bulky a yarn or else this could happen!

careful how you use your horizontal stripes otherwise you could end up looking like one of these three people.

Diagram 11
Before making the tension swatch on which you will base your first sweater, it is important to practise sewing in the cut off ends neatly. The simplest way to do this is to secure the ends in a series of reef knots as follows: tie the last cut thread of thin yarn to the first cut thread of thick yarn and the last cut end of thick yarn to the first cut thread of thin yarn and so on. Repeat until every loose thread is accounted for. Thread one pair at a time through a bodkin and weave the ends as invisibly and yet securely as possible into the body of the fabric. So far, so good. Now knit a perfect tension swatch. For this, I suggest 10 rows of mohair on alternate needles knitted on tension 10, followed by 10 rows of mercerized cotton on tension three. Because you are only using two yarns in this instance, there is no need to cut the threads at each changeover. Refer back to diagram 4. This is only necessary when you have two feeds and three yarns. After you have made this swatch, you are ready to knit your first sweater.

Diagram 12
Begin by counting the rows and stitches per 2.5cm (1in) on your sample and noting them down as you did in chapter 1. Next, study the photograph of the sweater shown on page 25. You will see that the cuffs of the garment are gathered – so is the hem! Thus the important measurements that you need to take are the width across the shoulders, the length of your body and arm and the depth of the armhole.

Diagram 13
Before noting these measurements down in your notebook, make sure that you understand the diagrammatic drawing of the garment. The body pieces of most sweaters are usually knitted from the hem to the shoulder and sleeves worked from the cuff to the shoulder. This design is different in that the body pieces are knitted from

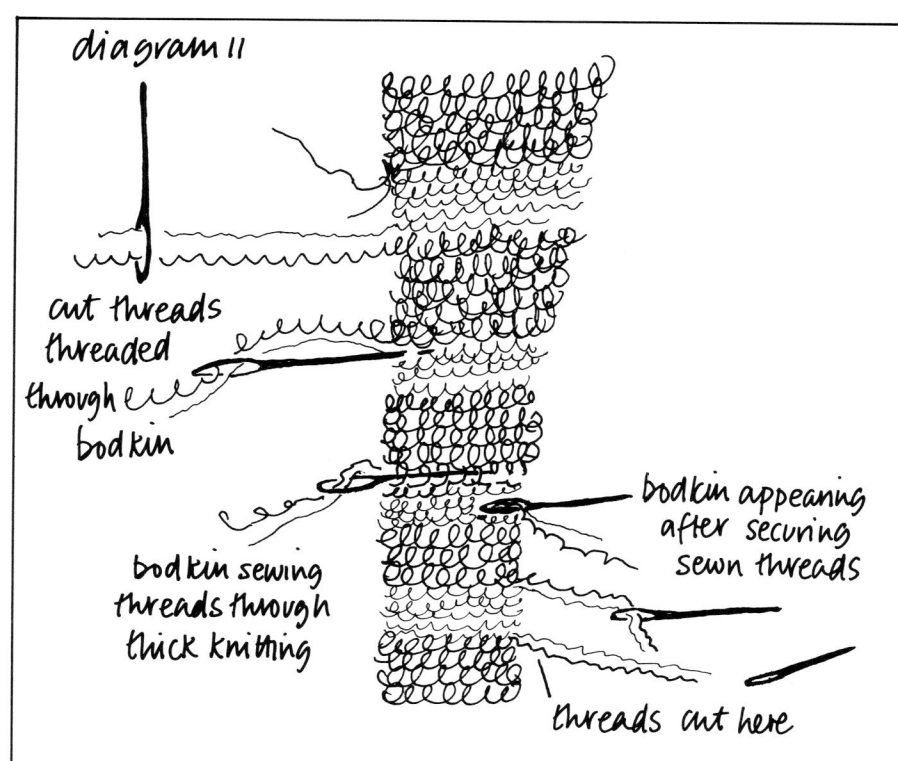

diagram 11

cut threads threaded through bodkin

bodkin sewing threads through thick knitting

bodkin appearing after securing sewn threads

threads cut here

side seam to side seam and the sleeves from side seam to side seam. There is no shaping. The back and front are two identical rectangles; so are the sleeves. Using the tension swatch and the notes you have made regarding your measurements, you can estimate the number of stitches to cast on and so knit two pieces for the front and back. Make two other pieces for sleeves. Check that each pair is identical, press them and sew and weave in any loose ends.

The next step is to make hems on the sleeves and front and back pieces. To do this, you must first check how many stitches there are on the rows of a tension swatch knitted in the fine yarn. Having made the necessary notes, measure yourself, deciding how loose you want the hem to be. Divide your findings by two for the correct number of needles on which to knit the hem.

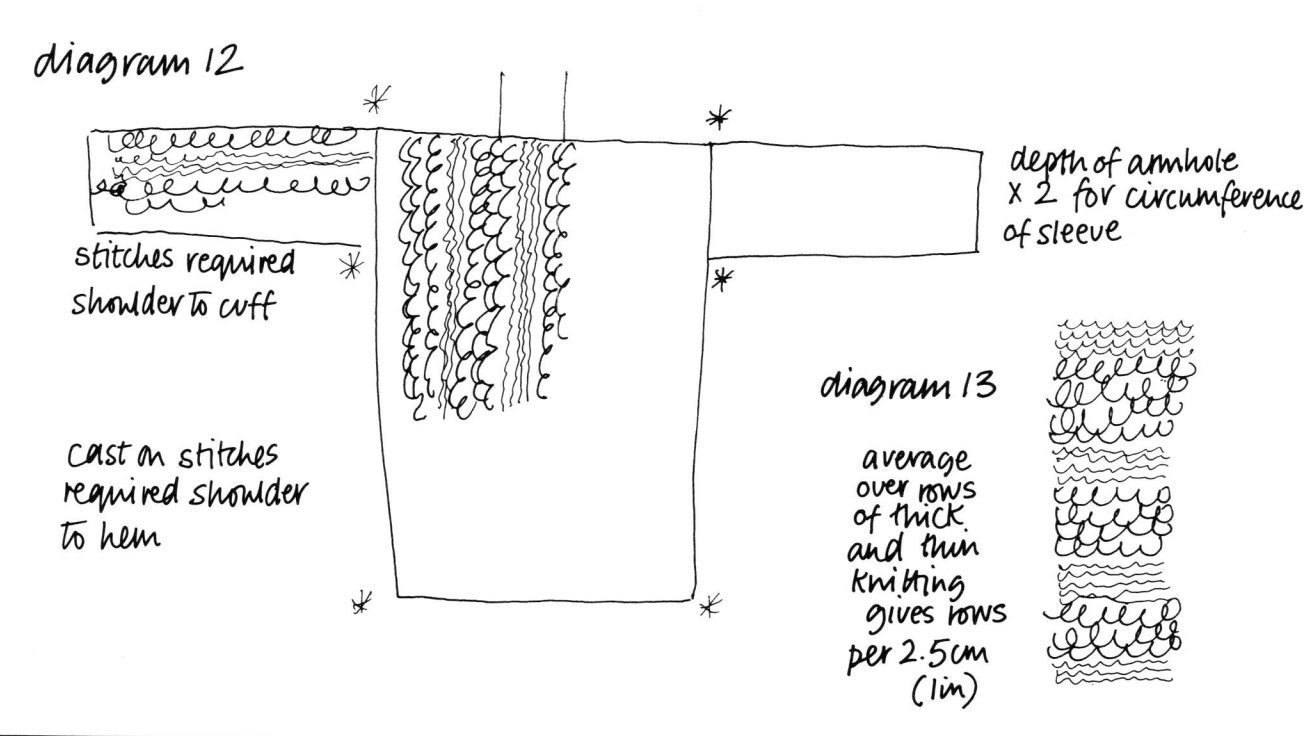

diagram 12

stitches required shoulder to cuff

cast on stitches required shoulder to hem

depth of armhole × 2 for circumference of sleeve

diagram 13

average over rows of thick and thin knitting gives rows per 2.5cm (1in)

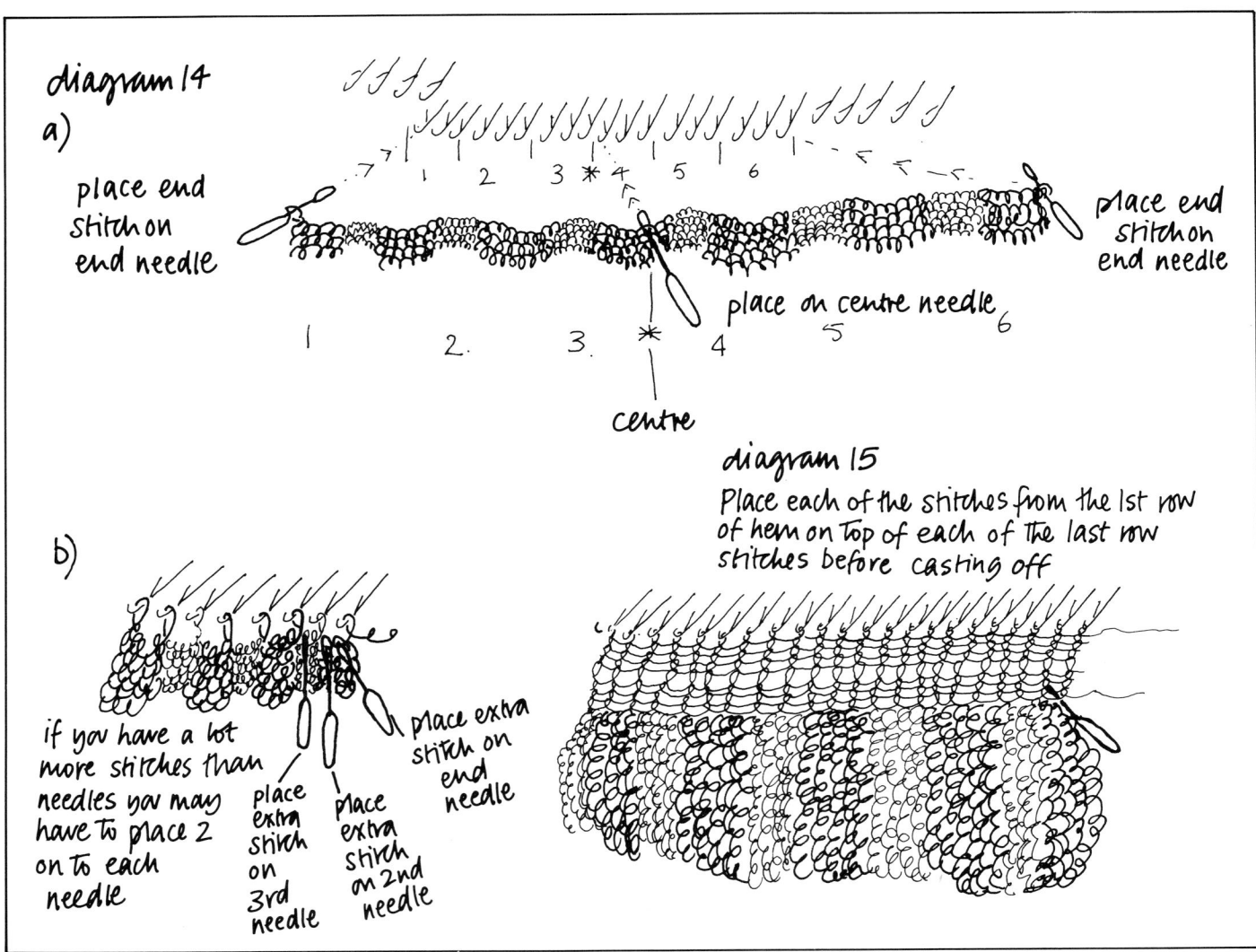

Diagram 14
Now place the bottom edge of the piece you designate as the front on to the number of needles that you require. The easiest way to do this is to mark your hem edge into eight equal parts – or 10, depending on how many needles you need for your hem (a).
Working in this way, you can ensure that your hem is cast on evenly. Divide up the needles in the same way you did for the hem edge. Pick up all the stitches on to the needles, noting that if you have a lot more stitches than needles, you may have to attach two stitches on to each needle (b).
With all the stitches picked up, thread the fine yarn and adjust the tension. Knit 10 rows for the hem, then one row at a looser tension. Change the tension dial to where it stood originally and knit another 10 rows.

Diagram 15
Pick up each of the cast-on stitches (the first row you knitted in fine yarn) and place them on the needles in action. Make sure you cast them on to the correct needles, looping the end stitch first of all and referring back to Monday's diagram if you need a further reminder of what to do.
Once all the stitches have been accounted for, cast them off two by two, remembering to loop the yarn around the adjacent needles as you do so.
Make another hem on the back piece in the same way.
For the sleeves, work out how wide you need your cuffs to be. Once you have this measurement and have worked out how many stitches you need to cast on, make the cuffs in the

same way as you did for the hems on the back and front pieces.
The next step is to create an edging for the neck of the sweater. Simply place every row as a stitch on to a needle, then, using the cotton, knit two hems, approximately 20 rows each, one for the back and the other for the front. Alter the dial to tension four and knit as for the previous hems. With this done, you are at last ready to sew your sweater together.

Diagram 16
Use a fine yarn, similar to the one with which you assembled your bandeau. Begin by laying the back and front pieces together so that the edges that form the shoulders and neck overlap and are together (a). Pin the sleeve head to the shoulder seam and then pin the back and front armhole to the body. Sew these pinned pieces together before pinning the side seams together from the armhole to the hem. Sew by hand, using the method explained on Monday's diagram. Pin the sleeves and sew the sleeve seams. Now only the shoulder seams are left. If you feel the neck is still too wide, continue the overlap, pinning to the point at which you feel comfortable (b). Before sewing, make sure it fits over your head. Sew each side equally to this mark.

Now put it on. It looks most attractive? Good. You feel you could go anywhere in it? Good. It reflects the restrained and understated mood you feel today? Good again.

Time then to begin another jersey: equally pretty, equally restrained. This one is not going to rely on hems for shaping; instead rouleaux threaded through a series of holes 5cm (2in) from the hem and cuff edges.
Unlike the holes and rouleaux employed on Monday, however, these are going to serve a distinctly practical purpose: gathering the fabric into the waist and around the wrists. Refer back to Monday's diagram for clarification if necessary.

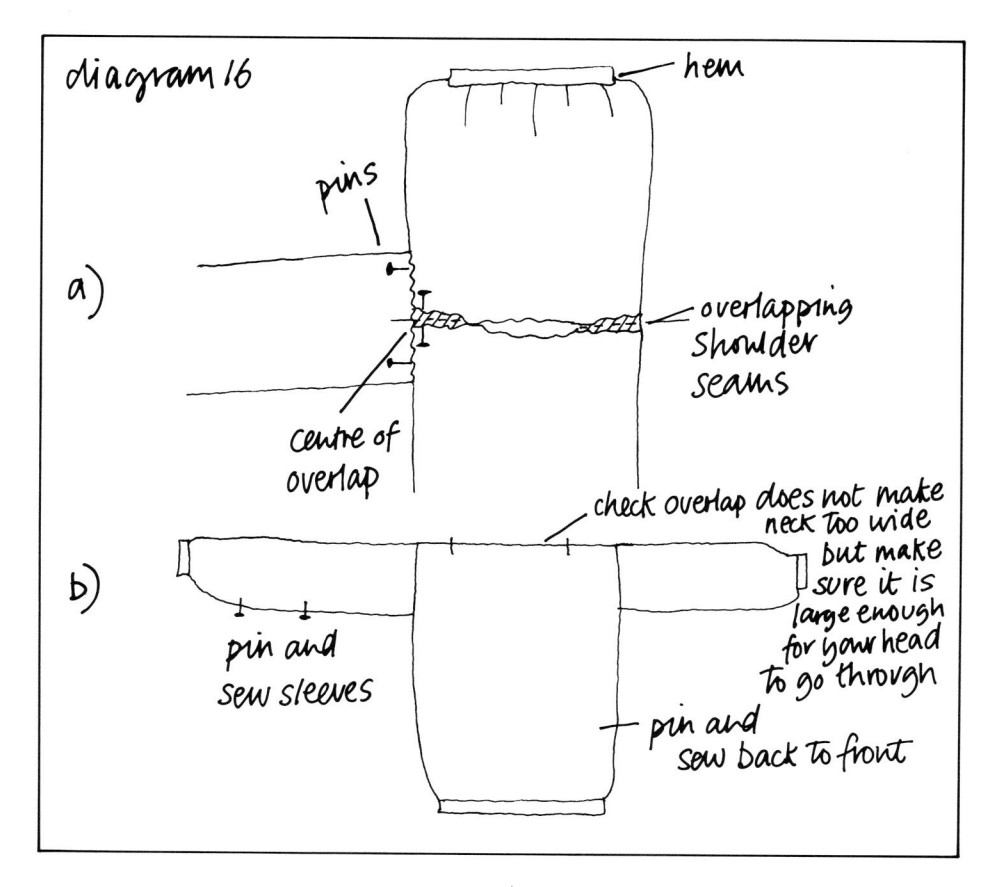

Just as for the first sweater, a tension swatch is necessary. On this second, however, perhaps you would like to try knitting the ridges horizontally rather than vertically. If you decide on this, do not choose a bulky yarn; you could end up looking like a Michelin man! You may also wish to vary your thin yarns just as you did with the thicker ones used for the first design. If you do, choose a thin yarn similar in weight to the first.

Begin by counting the stitches per 2.5cm (1in) for the width and the rows per 2.5cm (1in) for the depth.
Cast on the number of stitches you require for the front and knit the number of rows necessary for the correct length, stopping 5cm (2in) before you reach the edge to be cast off. Now, every eight stitches, transfer the eighth on to the adjacent needle just as you did in Monday's diagram. Having pushed the vacated needle out of action, knit two rows. Now bring the needle back into the knitting position and continue to knit until you reach the edge. Instead of casting off, try a 5cm (2in) hem in an even finer yarn (altering the tension accordingly). Knowing how many stitches there are to every 5cm (2in) in this yarn, knit the required number of rows, including one at a looser tension to form the fold-line. Then pick up the first row of the hem in the usual way and cast off. Repeat for the back.

For the sleeves, begin at the cuff edges with a hem in one of your fine yarns. Knit the same number of rows as you have just done on the front and back hems, transferring stitches to form holes and then continuing to knit until you reach the shoulder seam.

35

diagram 18

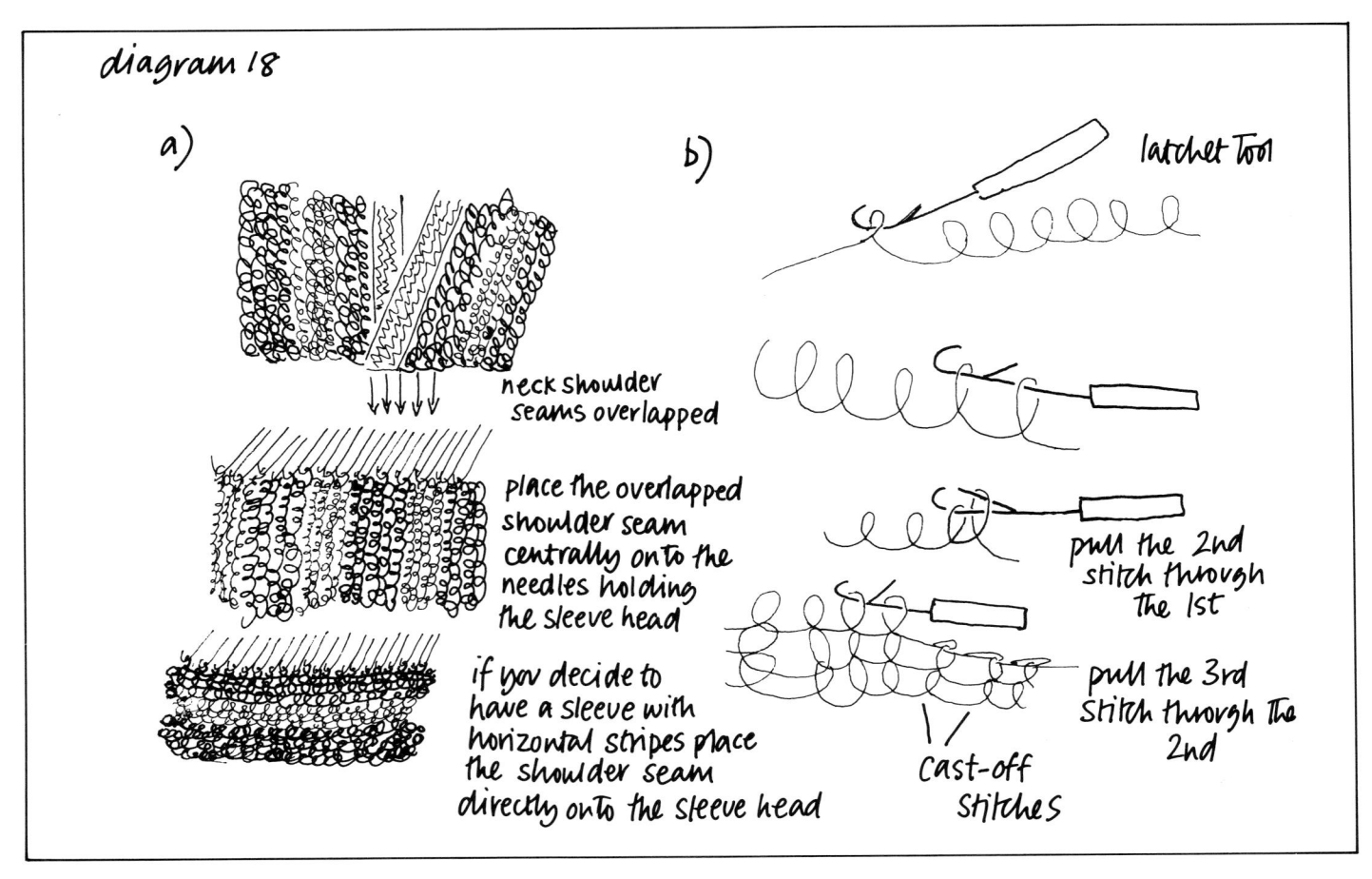

a) neck shoulder seams overlapped

place the overlapped shoulder seam centrally on to the needles holding the sleeve head

if you decide to have a sleeve with horizontal stripes place the shoulder seam directly on to the sleeve head

b) latchet tool

pull the 2nd stitch through the 1st

pull the 3rd stitch through the 2nd

cast-off stitches

Diagram 18
In exactly the same way as you did for the first sweater, overlap the shoulder seams to form the neckline and then place the centre of the overlapped edge to the centre of the needles (a). Place equal amounts of the front and back shoulder seam stitches on to the remaining needles in action. Cast off the stitches together (b). Alternatively, you could sew the sleeves and armholes by hand.
Repeat for the other sleeve head.
Now it is time to knit the rouleau. Emphasize the whole design rather than the separate parts by making it all in the same yarn and as one length. Cast on and start knitting. Keep knitting; you will need miles of it. Cast off and remove from the machine. After assembling the sweater, cut the rouleau into four pieces, finishing off any loose ends by hand. Thread them through the holes as shown in the illustration opposite.
Now you have your second subtle and pretty sweater to wear for Tuesday.

Diagram 19
Hopefully you are already becoming aware of the improvisations you can make on these two basic designs; if not, perhaps I can recommend a few ways in which you can combine the techniques learned so far in this chapter before Tuesday is over.

Try: a plain body and patterned sleeves; a series of vertical holes to create a pattern rather than making them horizontally; gathering the hem on the machine rather than using a rouleau to do the job; creating horizontal ridges rather than vertical. Having made two very ridged sweaters, how about trying one with less surface texture? Experiment with stripes of contrasting yarns; the effects achieved can be most attractive. After all, subtlety and restraint are the mood of the day and the neutral tones in contrasting yarns will provide a perfect vehicle for the expression of this feeling.
If you are exhausted or do not have the time to do all this straight away, stick all the yarns you think would work together in your sketch book to try out at some later date. After all, all this restraint is probably becoming a little tedious and you will want a change tomorrow. This is just what I have in mind.

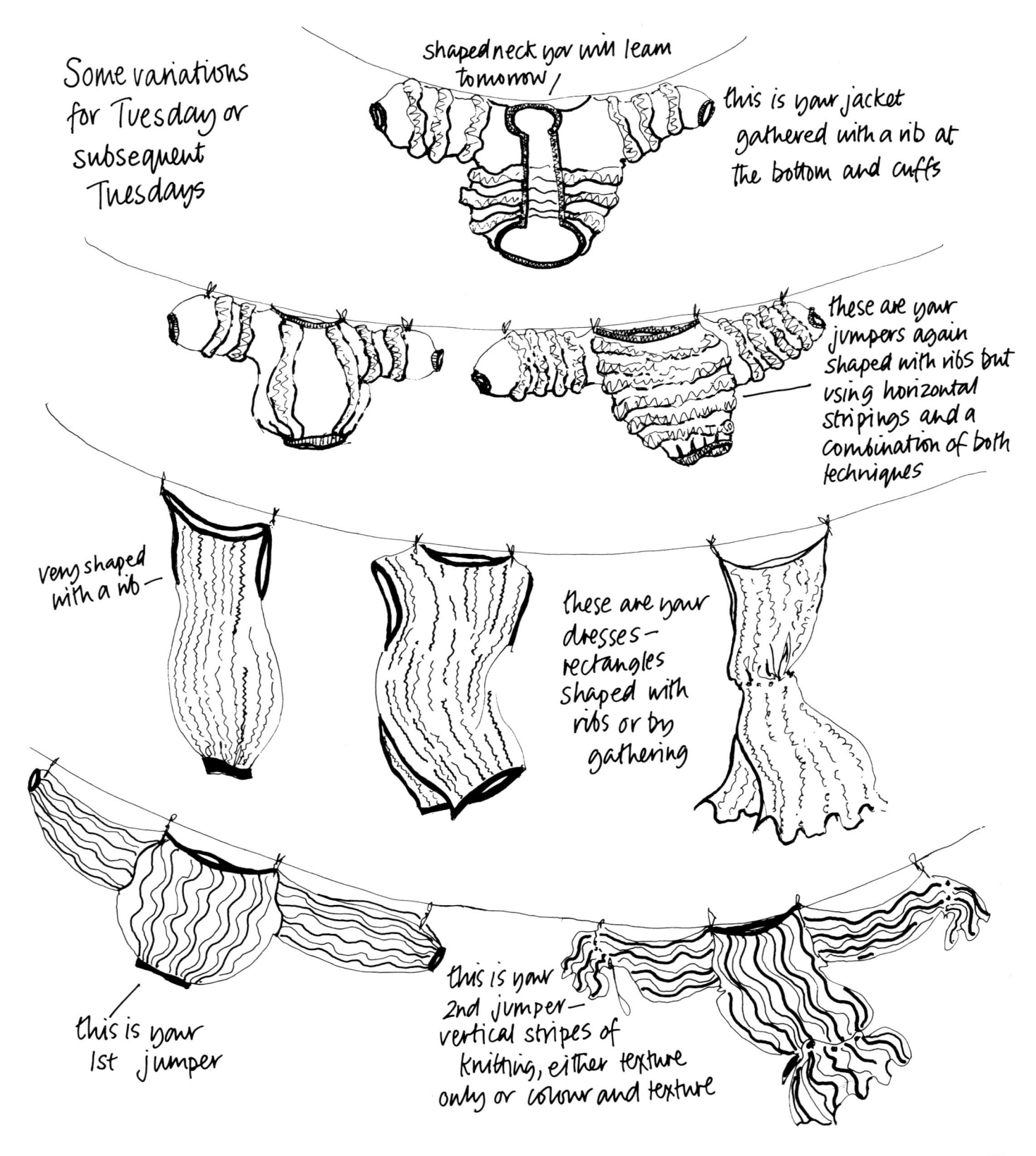

Some variations for Tuesday or subsequent Tuesdays

shaped neck you will learn tomorrow

this is your jacket gathered with a rib at the bottom and cuffs

these are your jumpers again shaped with ribs but using horizontal stripings and a combination of both techniques

very shaped with a rib

these are your dresses — rectangles shaped with ribs or by gathering

this is your 1st jumper

this is your 2nd jumper — vertical stripes of knitting, either texture only or colour and texture

Wednesday

After the self-enforced restraint of Tuesday, you probably want a complete contrast: to feel and look really flamboyant. No longer diffident in your approach to knitting, you find your mood today – Wednesday – one of creative exuberance; you are consumed by an overwhelming desire to make something far more ambitious than Monday's bandeau, and far more colourful than Tuesday's understated sweater. This project will therefore combine all the colours of the last two days – and many of the techniques you have tried and tested too. The result? A dramatic and immensely striking sweater dress that can also be worn as a tunic over a skirt or jeans, in a range of such beautiful and unusual colours that it will fulfil your needs and new mood exactly. I shall also be making it up using the wrong side of the fabric and so that the seams show.

Not only will I be explaining how to make the dress, but again suggesting ways in which you can vary the basic design. However, in the excitement of anticipation, do not forget to keep referring back where necessary for techniques explained fully in preceding chapters, for I shall only be introducing two new techniques today: weaving in and shaping. On Monday you experimented weaving rouleaux through knitted fabric; today I shall be explaining how to weave yarns, ribbons and rouleaux *without* removing the knitting from the machine.

One final point: if you consider shaping too daunting at this stage, you can always create a woven fabric for the basic shapes of the previous chapter.

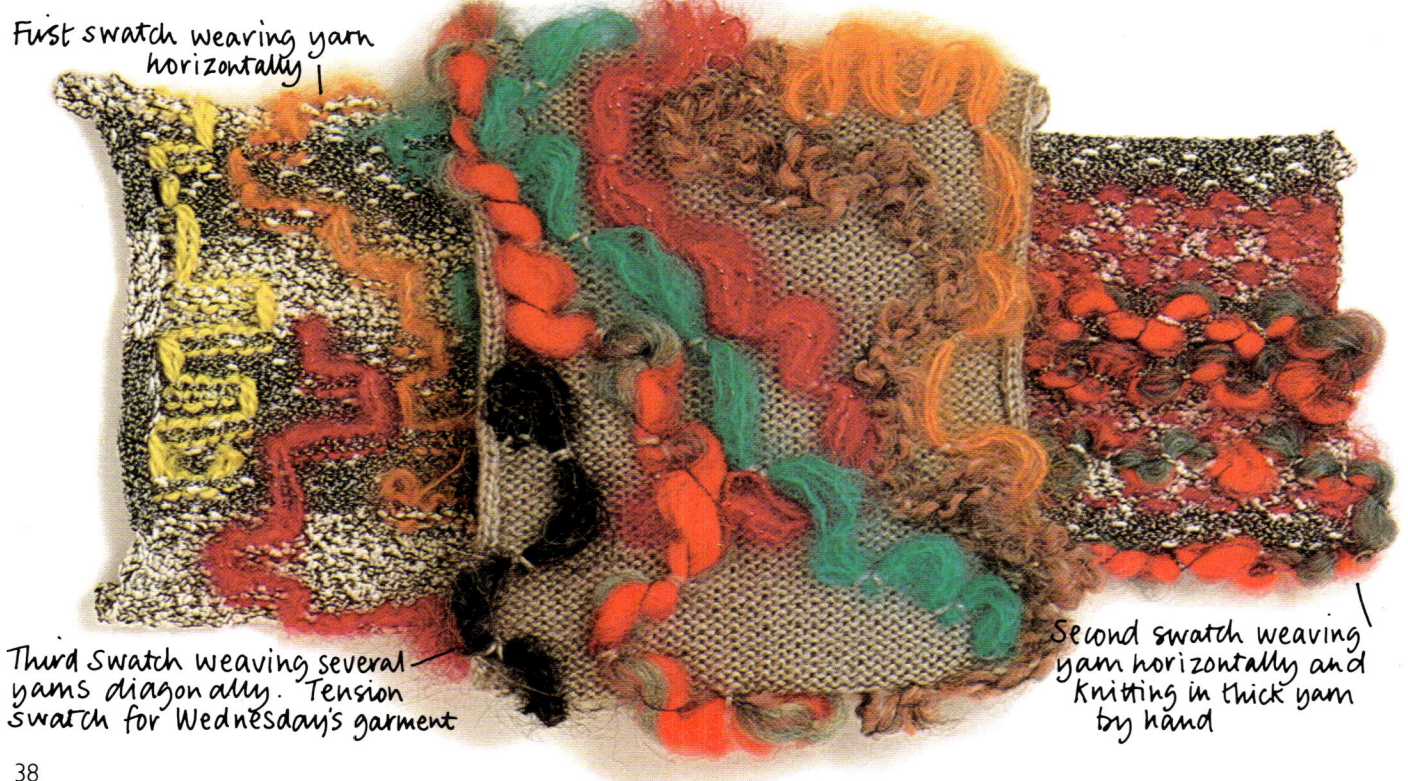

First swatch weaving yarn horizontally

Third swatch weaving several yarns diagonally. Tension swatch for Wednesday's garment

Second swatch weaving yarn horizontally and knitting in thick yarn by hand

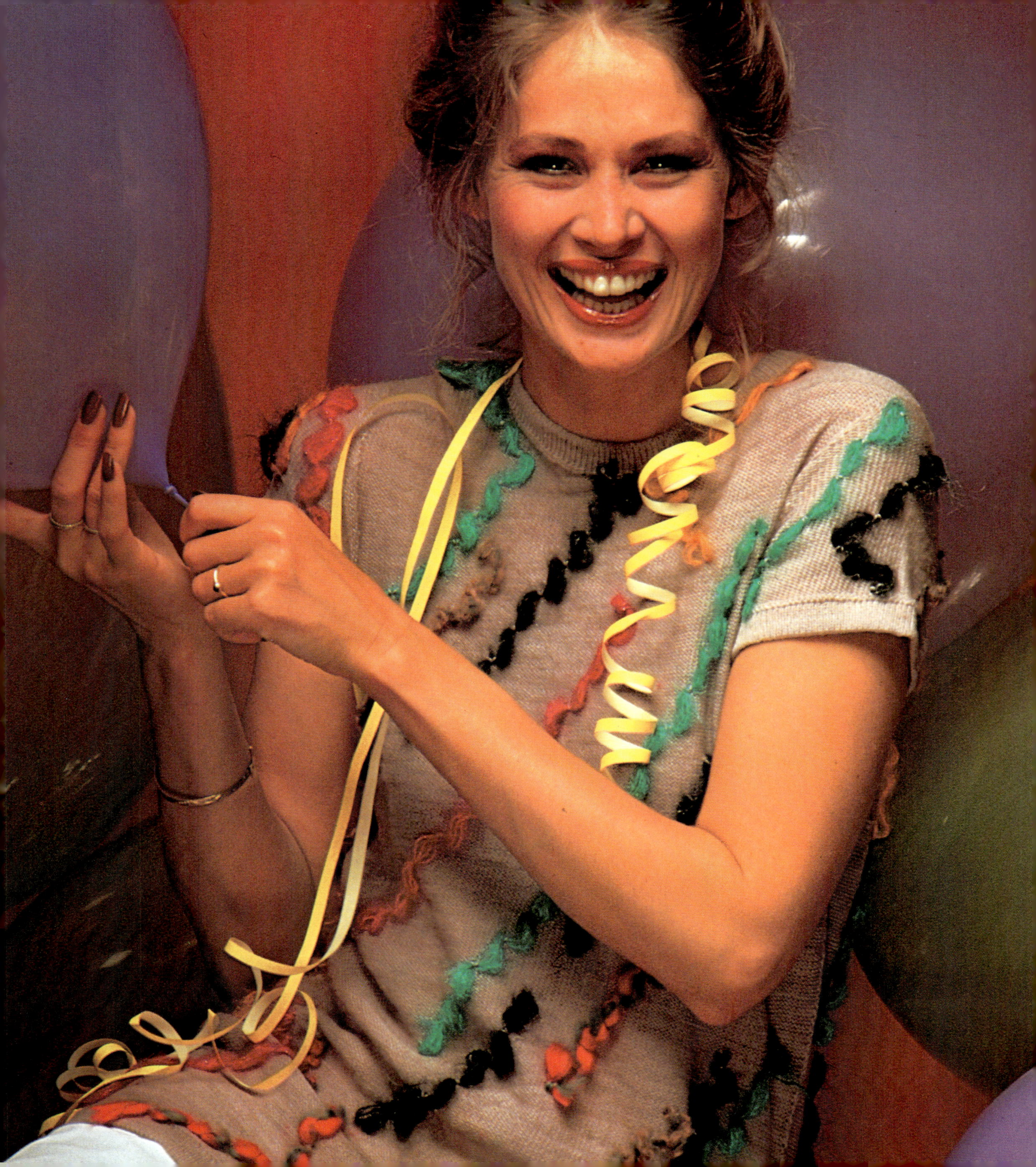

Diagram 1

thick twisted wool

uneven thick and thin wool slub

mohair

twisted black and white knopped yarn

very fat loosely-twisted soft wool

mohair twisted with lurex thread

diagram 2

a) texture using thick yarn at tension 10 and thin yarn at tension 4 in sequence

note edge curling to form ridges

b) different textured yarns at same tension producing fabric without accentuated ridges

Diagram 1
Having recovered from the overwhelming initial excitement of the proposed project, you must now settle down and be practical.
You probably still have the neutral yarns of diverse textures used in the previous project in front of you. Now collect, just as you did for the neutral yarns, as many textured yarns in different colours that you can find. You also need to pick out one or two black and white 'high twist' or 'knopped' yarns for background contrast. This time, you will not be restricted by the gauge of your machine: the yarns are to be 'laid' in, not knitted.
However, you will obviously not be able to use *all* of the yarns you have found, so select a range that you think will look striking together and then restrict yourself to the number indicated in the photograph – that is about six . You may decide on only four or even less if they are space - dyed a technique of dipping skeins of yarn into different dyes for multi – coloured yarns.

Diagram 2
By now you should be completely familiar with the method of making tension swatches – and the need to do so. Thread the machine with any two of

40

the neutral yarns or black and white yarns: they can vary in texture, tone and colour, but not weight.
Unlike Tuesday's knitting, where the neutrals alone form the texture, here they are used to provide a background surface on to which contrasting textured yarns will be superimposed. You will be doing this by weaving in a variety of different yarns as you actually knit the main fabric of the swatch – and later, the garment itself. With the machine threaded correctly, cast on to a suitable number of needles for your first tension swatch. Knit 10 rows at a tension appropriate to the two neutral yarns you are using. Then change to the second yarn and knit another 10 rows. Now, holding the knitting down with one hand – or preferably securing it with weights – push out all the needles.

Diagram 3

Select one of the coloured textured yarns: a fuchsia mohair with a silver twist running through it would be an admirable choice. Weave this under and over pairs of pushed out needles as indicated. Before taking the carriage across the needles, make sure that it is programmed (refer to your manual) to knit needles in this pushed out position, otherwise the carriage will fail to knit. Knit three rows, then another six before changing over to the neutral yarn. Push out the needles and weave in the mohair as before. Knit three rows. Repeat this procedure several times, and you will notice that the mohair is forming a rather interesting pattern. At least, it should be!

Diagram 4

Change now to the second neutral yarn and knit several rows. If your experiments with the mohair have been successful, why not try a complete contrast – a thick twisted space-dyed yarn, for example? In order to weave this successfully, you will find it easier to bring out three needles at a time.

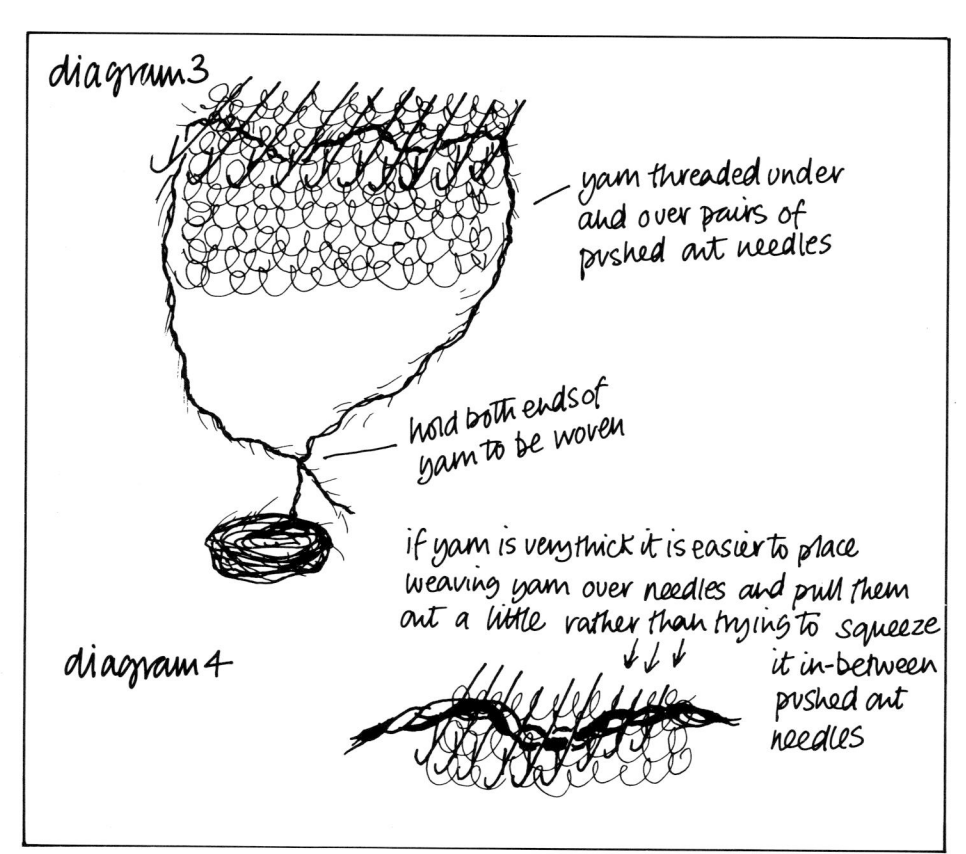

Wind the yarn over the first three, bring out the second three, wind the yarn under, bring out the third set of three, wind the yarn over, and so on. If the yarn is too thick and bulky, it could get caught between individual needles and not fit properly.

Knit several rows using this technique, then repeat in the opposite direction. Change the neutral yarn, knit several rows, weave a row with the mohair, knit more rows and then weave a row with the bulky yarn as has just been described. Continue knitting, changing your neutral yarns roughly every 10 rows, alternately weaving the mohair and your bulky yarn. When you consider the knitting constitutes a swatch, cast off. Press the edges only, so that you do not flatten the woven rows.

I hope these experiments have not proved too confusing; if your knitting looks anything like the swatch shown in the first photograph, you have done really well. I shall assume it does.

For your next swatch, weave in three – even four – coloured textured yarns, either in conjunction with one another or separately. This time, however, try weaving them in diagonally instead of horizontally. This may sound alarming; really it is quite easy.

Begin by cutting lengths of the weaving yarns you propose using: they will be much easier to handle. Allow about 30.5cm (12in) of each yarn for the swatch. If you do not cut lengths of yarn, you are in danger of finding it wrapped around everything. This is a very irritating predicament and to be avoided at all costs. With the cut lengths on the table beside you, cast on your first row in neutral yarn. Knit 10 rows as before, then change to the second neutral yarn and knit another few rows. Check that your weights are well secured.

diagram 5

a) cut length of thick textured yarn held over pushed out needles before knitting

b) hold loop of yarn formed from 1st woven-in stitch and cut end ready for knitting in

c) pull down loop of yarn and cut end ready to change direction

diagram 6

d) changing direction of weaving yarn

a) 2nd yarn woven in horizontally / 1st yarn woven in diagonally

b) diagonally woven-in yarn crossing over horizontally woven in yarn

Diagram 5

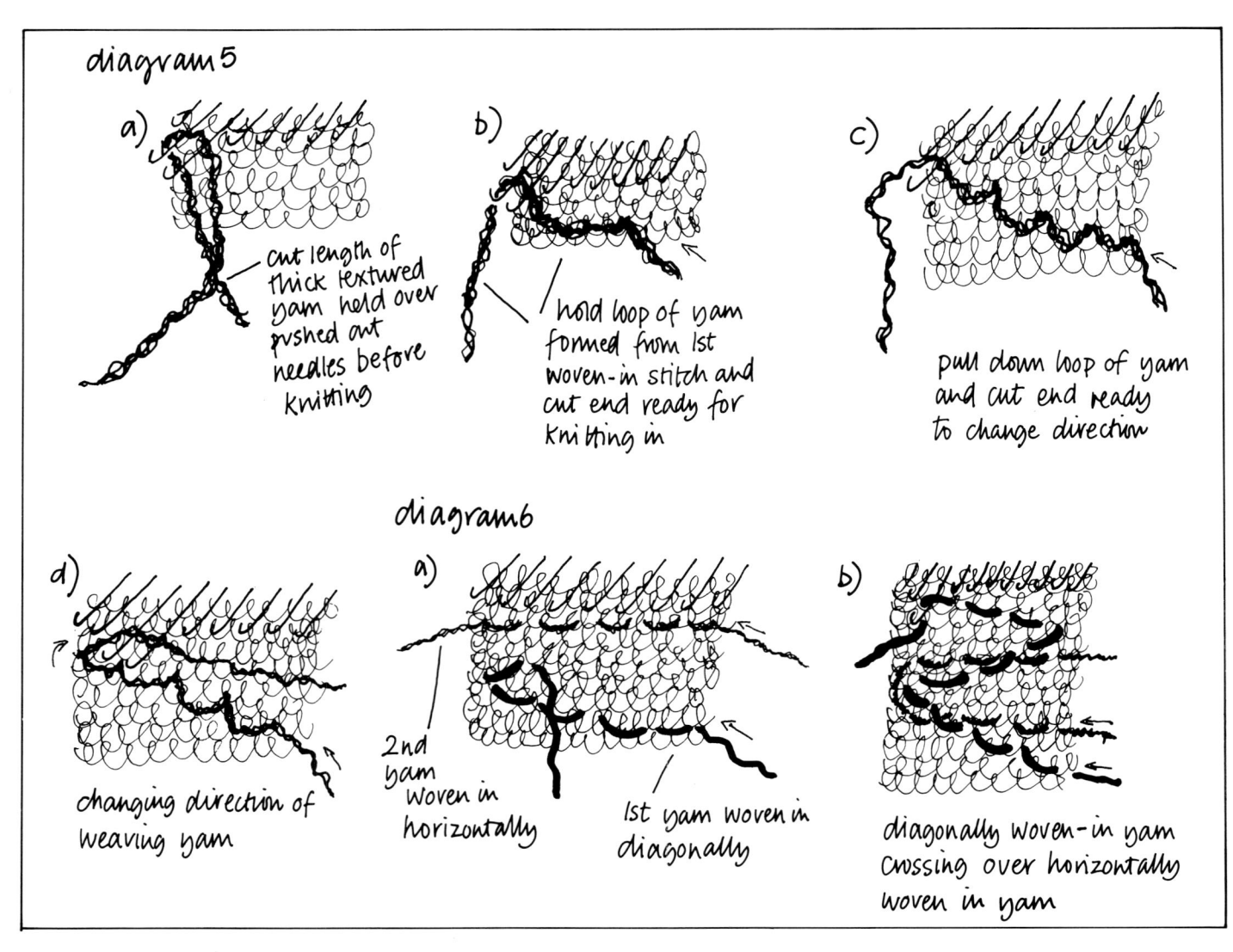

Select a length of thick textured yarn – a slub perhaps. Place over one or two pushed out needles; hold both ends so that it does not bounce off the needle when you take the carriage across (a). After four rows, pull out another needle about 2.5cm (1in) along from the first one, place the thick yarn over the needle, pinch the loop and the loose end together under the needle and knit four more rows (b). Repeat this procedure several times, until you reach the other side of the swatch. At this point, change to the second neutral yarn and knit several rows. Pick up the thick slub yarn again and loop it in the opposite direction starting with a needle on the edge (c and d). Before knitting it in, choose another yarn – why not an emerald green mohair, for example. Use this doubled, even trebled. Pull out a needle on the other side of the swatch and loop the doubled or trebled ends on to it. Hold the loose end out of the way – and you are ready to knit again. Knit several rows, repeating the looping and knitting one yarn at a time. You have to do this, because having only one pair of hands, it is impossible to hold each yarn separately in place as you take the carriage across.

Diagram 6

Having looped and knitted with both yarns over several rows, you are now faced with a choice before taking the next step. Either cross the mohair and slub yarn over, or make each one change direction (a and b).
Once you are confident that you can weave in two directions diagonally, try adding a third and fourth yarn.

Oh dear – too many yarns!

Do be careful, however, as it is not difficult to find yourself in the unhappy predicament of the knitter illustrated.

Diagram 7

Nearing the end of knitting up this swatch, you will need to know how to secure the ends of the woven threads. If the yarn is quite thick, simply cut it close to the last woven-in stitch. If, on the other hand, the yarn looks as if it might slip through the woven stitch, twist it around the last pushed out needle before knitting that row and then cut it. If you prefer, remove the swatch from the machine, press the edges and then cut off the loose ends afterwards.

Diagram 8

Now that you have successfully completed two thoroughly textured and extravagantly coloured swatches, it is perhaps a good idea to experiment with a few more combinations of horizontal and diagonal weaving (a, b and c). Instead of using the same two neutral yarns for the background, try some alternatives – or one on its own perhaps.

Now take a good look at all the swatches you have made. Hopefully there will be one that you would like to use as the basis for your sweater dress; I think it only fair after all that work that you should go right ahead and make it now.

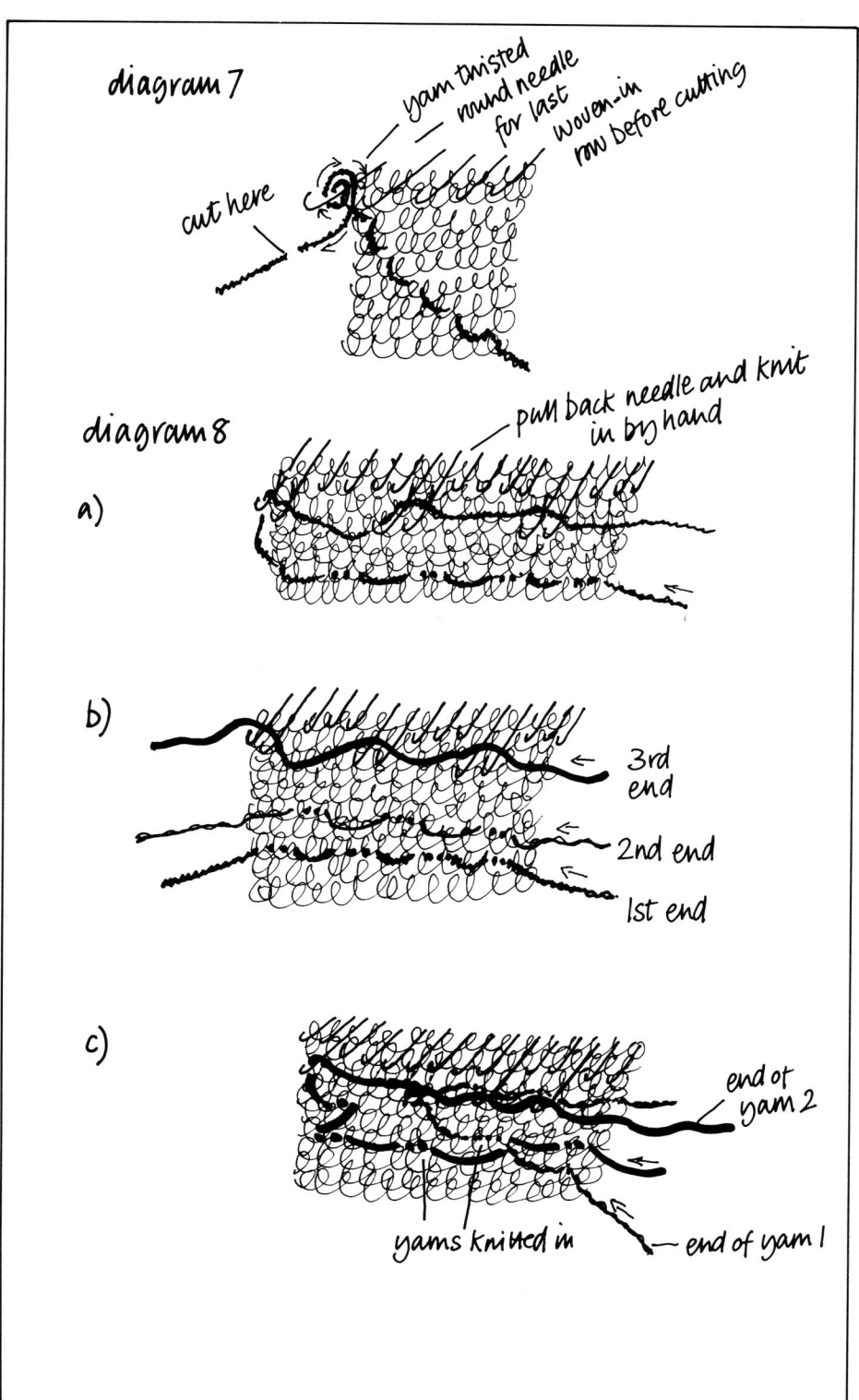

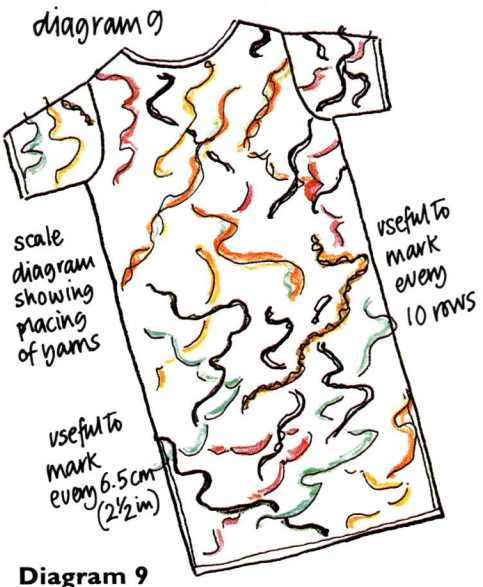

Diagram 9
Note down the rows and stitches per 2.5cm (1in) to establish the tension of the swatch you want to use. Then make a drawing, or rather a large diagram, of the proposed design. Crayon on the colours, directions and thicknesses or weights of the yarns with which you intend to weave. You could alternatively stick lengths of the yarns you want to use in place with clear tape – although if they are expensive this might be rather wasteful.

Diagram 10
Mark the armhole (a), neck (b) and back opening (c) and their measurements, noting that the back neck is higher than at the front and the back armhole deeper than the front. There are two ways you can cope with these discrepancies. One is to ignore them completely until you come to sew the garment together and then cut the surplus away after marking the line with a row of zigzag machine stitching – called the 'cut and sew' method. However, this can be difficult, or at its worst, disastrous, because it is so easy to pull the knitting out of shape during the machining stage.

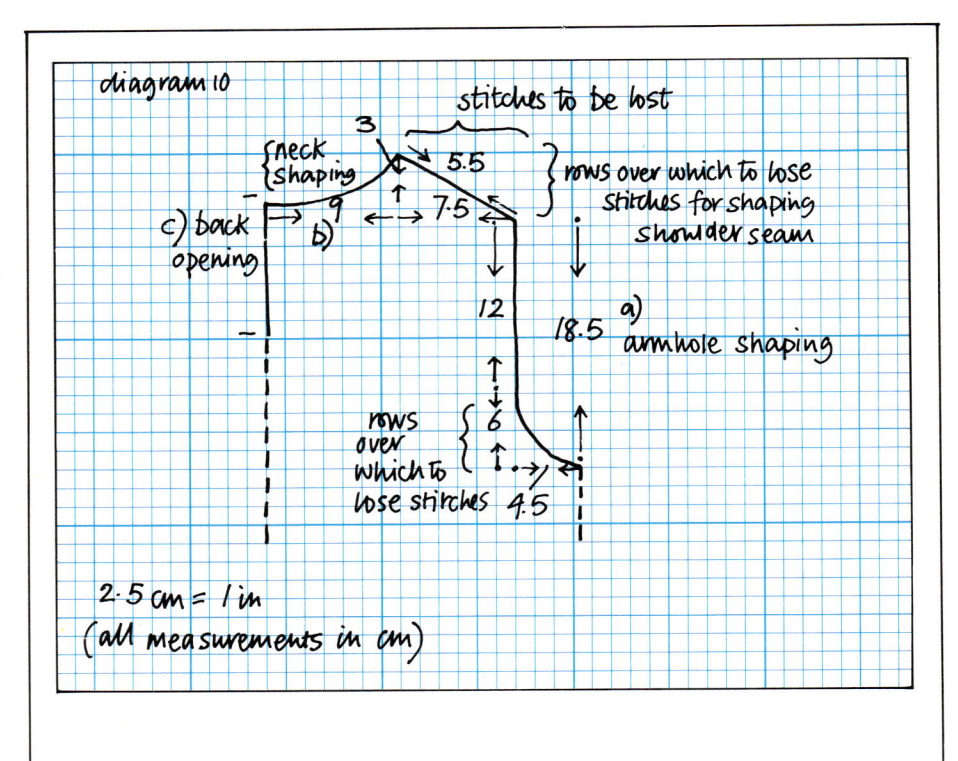

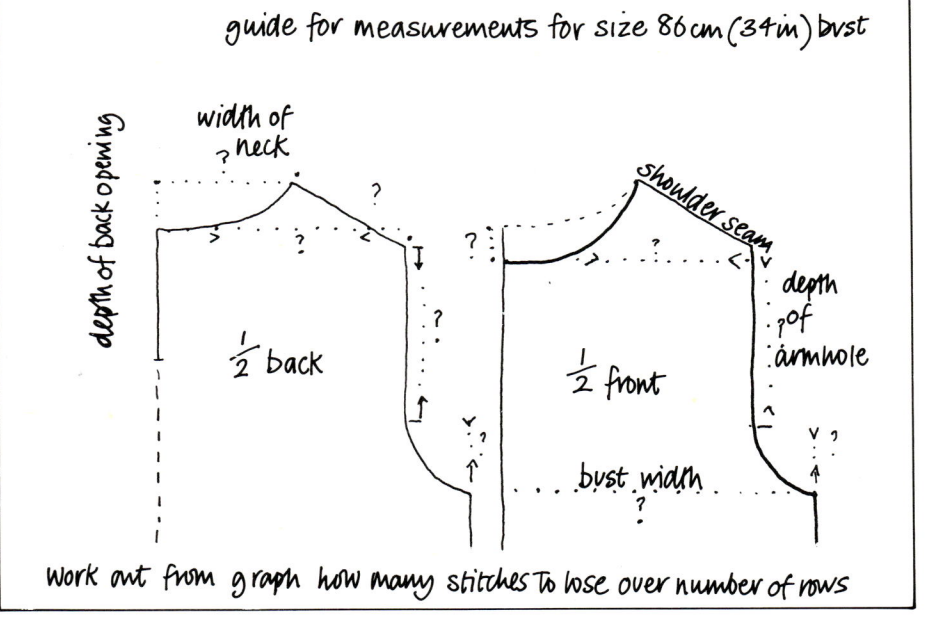

So rather than risk the responsibility of ruining a beautiful sweater I propose to show how you can shape the individual pieces that make up the design on your knitting machine. Having taken your measurements and decided on the size you want the sweater to be, cast on as many stitches as you know you will require for half your hip measurement for the front. Knit a hem 21 rows in depth (including the fold-line), then begin to knit the straight length of the front, weaving in your selected yarns according to the directions and colours given on the scale drawing.

Diagram 11

You know the measurement between the hem and armhole so, long before you reach the latter point, check that the weaving will not interfere with the decreasing that you are about to begin. You should have worked out in advance how many stitches you need to lose for the front and back armholes, remembering that you will be decreasing rather more on the back than the front.

Do not forget that, during decreasing (a, b and c), you must decrease evenly on both sides, otherwise the armholes will be uneven. You should need to decrease no more than five stitches on each side, but do not forget that during this decreasing, you must continue weaving according to your scale drawing.

Remember one other thing: keep the weaving yarns well out of the way of the decreasing on the edges.

With the correct number of stitches decreased and the formation of the shaped armholes successfully achieved, continue to knit happily, weaving as you go, until you reach the neckline. Here, instead of decreasing on both sides simultaneously, you will have to knit one half of the neckline first, then the other.

Diagram 12

Begin by finding the centre of the front piece. Bring out all the needles to one side of this point, then make a note of the number on the row counter because you will have to return to the same place for the other half of the neck once the first is completed.

For this part of the garment, it is imperative that you programme your carriage to knit only those needles that are in the knitting position, not those pushed right out.

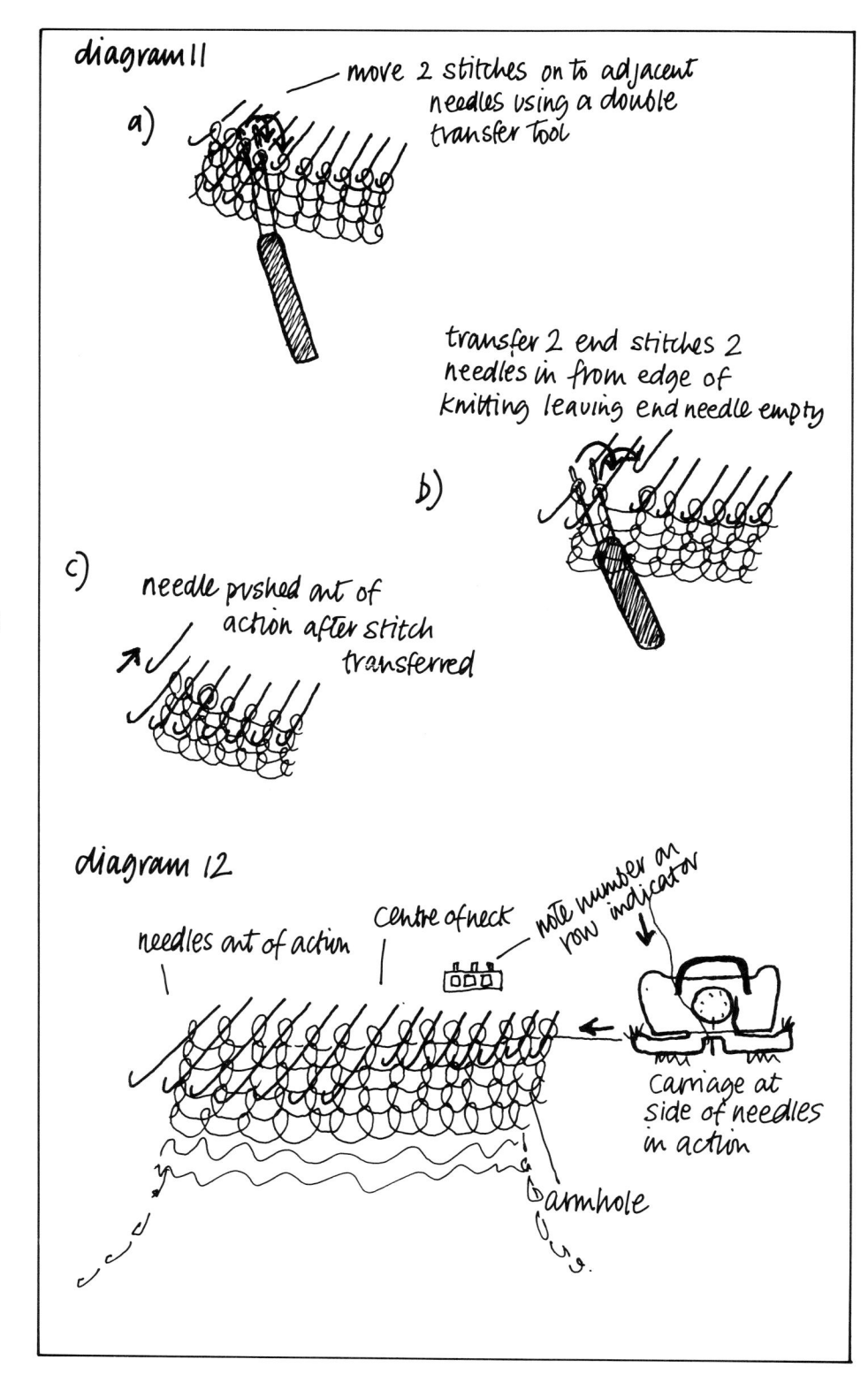

Two tunics

different coloured mohairs woven in diagonally on machine

longer undecorated tunic under woven-in open cardigan

tight mauve silky-knit trousers

open-knit footless tights

Diagram 13
If you need to continue weaving the surface pattern during this stage – and I hope you can avoid this – you will have to pull out, very slightly, the needles with which you are weaving, otherwise they will just not knit.

Diagram 14
Before knitting this section, you must not only establish where the centre of the neck lies (a), but also where the neckline will end (b). Count the needles from each end and note down the two sets of numbers of each as far as the point where the neckline will end.

Diagram 15
Knit two rows and push out two needles at the centre. Knit another two rows and push out two needles. Knit two and push out another two, and so on (a). Continue in this way until you have knitted the right number of rows (according to your estimate) for the correct depth of the neck. This point should coincide with the beginning of the shoulder (b); if it does not, there is no need to worry; it will be near enough.
Before knitting the other side of the neck and shoulder, turn the row counter back to where it was before you started the first half. You made a note in your book, remember?

Diagram 16
Push out all the needles, take the carriage across to the other side of the machine, push out all the needles on the side of the machine on which you have just knitted the first half of the neck. Now cut the yarn and secure it to the clamp on the side on which you will be knitting for the second half. Now knit the second side as you did for the first, but in reverse, decreasing and weaving according to your scale drawing.

Diagram 17
When you have done this, do not cast

diagram 13 — pull needle out only a little with weaving yarn placed over it

diagram 14 — shoulder begins here (a); neck (b); centre neck; neck (b); shoulder begins here. Note down number of needles for shoulders and neck.

diagram 15 a) 1st 2 rows; 2nd 2 rows; 3rd 2 rows

b) shoulder needles / neck needles / shoulder needles

diagram 16 — tie on to clamp

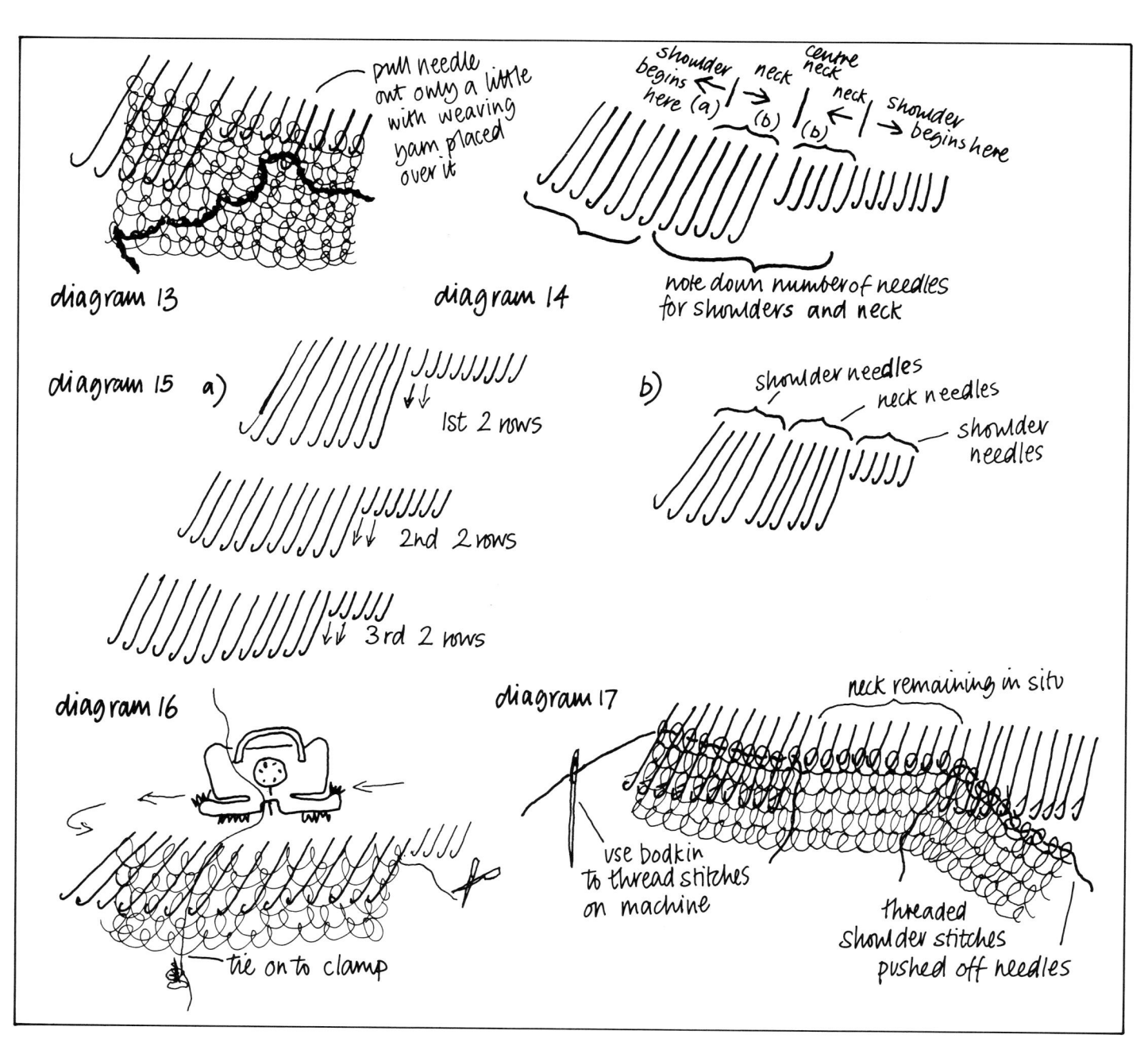

diagram 17 — neck remaining in situ; use bodkin to thread stitches on machine; threaded shoulder stitches pushed off needles

off. Instead, thread a bodkin with thin coloured yarn – preferably one that is slippery so that it can be removed easily later on – and then thread it through all the stitches remaining that form one shoulder.
Slip off the needles all the stitches through which you have run a thread, then do the same with the other shoulder.
Finally, using a different coloured thread, slip the bodkin through the stitches that form the neck and remove them from the needles.
Hold the completed front up against you. It should look most striking.

It does? Excellent. Now you can go ahead and knit the back.
Knitting this second piece should prove a great deal easier than the first because you know now the problems you may encounter and have experience of dealing with them.

47

Diagram 18

The main difference here is that when you start increasing, about 20 rows before reaching the shoulder seam, you will need to knit this section in two parts in order to create a slit at the back through which you can put your head. This means that from the middle of the armhole depth, you have to knit one half at a time, just as you did for the front neckline. One point: remember to push out some needles for the depth of the neck. Thread the shoulders and neck with coloured threads just as you did on the front.

Diagram 19

With the front and back complete, it is time to knit the sleeves. You undoubtedly remember the principles of casting on the sleeve head and the armhole on the machine from Tuesday's project in chapter 2; you use the same method here. Note that you will be again knitting the sleeves from the sleeve head to the hem. Place the shoulder seam of the front and the back either side of the centre of the machine and place all the armhole stitches on the needles.

Diagram 20

To knit the sleeve head, hold the needles in exactly the same way that you held them for the shoulders. First, however, knit the central section, bringing out needles at each side every time you knit a row (a). While knitting the sleeve head, the carriage should be correctly programmed to knit only those needles that are in a knitting position, not those that are pushed right out. As you knit the sleeve head, all the needles will gradually come into action (b), then continue to knit straight for the correct length. Make a hem about 2.5cm (1in) deep, then cast off.

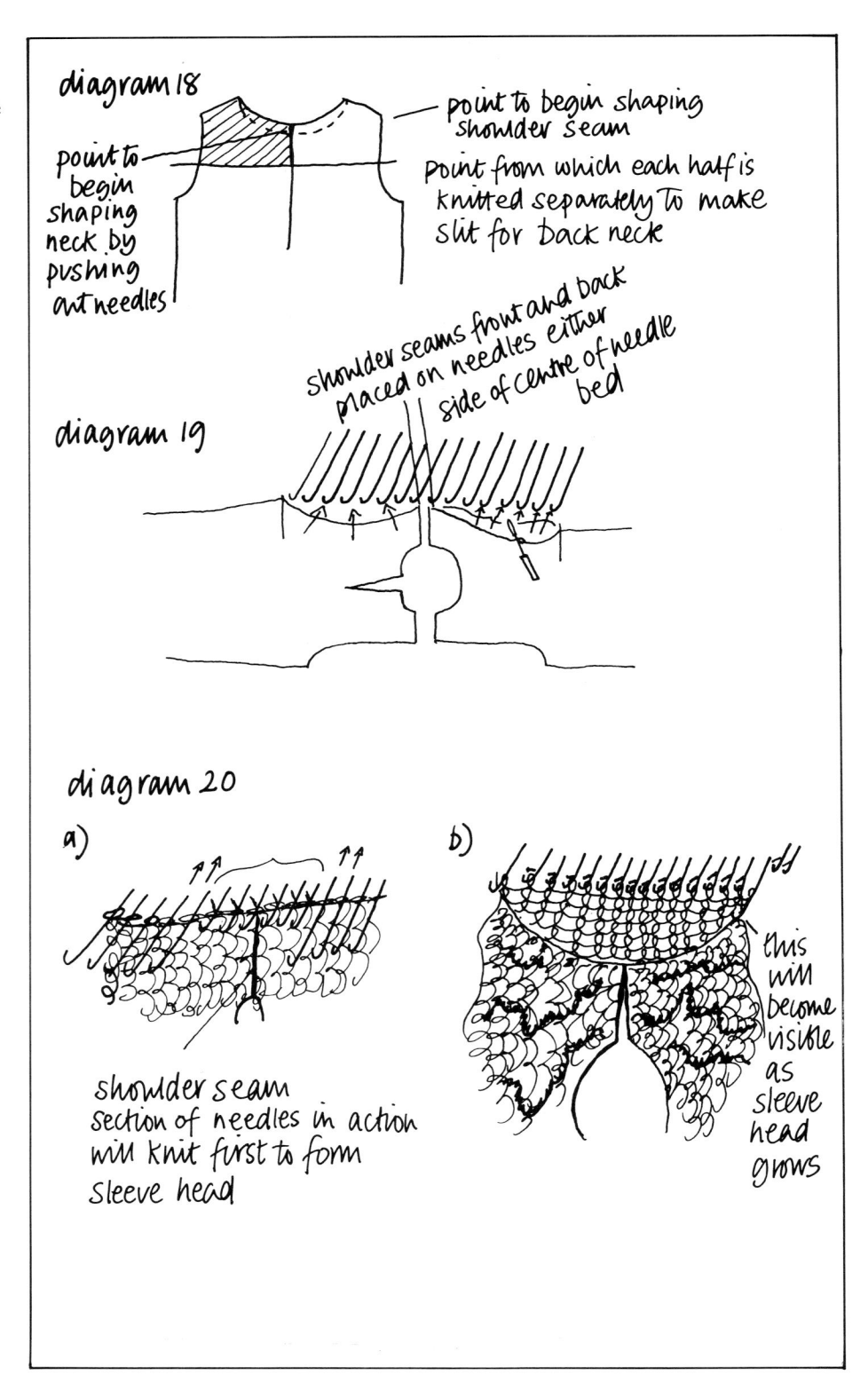

Make the second sleeve in the same way. At this point, you will be very relieved to hear that there is only a little more to do: casting off the shoulder seams and making hems at the neck and on the edges of the side slits at the hem.

Diagram 21
For the front neck, and with the work inside out so that the wrong side is facing you, place the neck stitches on to the machine. Once the stitches have been transferred to the needles, pull out the coloured threads and knit a hem, just as you did for the cuffs in the previous project (see page 35). Do the same for each half of the back neck, and cast off.
For the side slits, decide how high you want them to reach and then, with the wrong sides facing you, cast the sides on to the right number of needles without straining the knitting and make hems to the same depth as those on the neck; make each of the four hems on the sides the same length and depth. Now only the shoulder seams are left.

Diagram 22
Do you remember casting off (or grafting) seams together in the previous project?
Either refer back to page 36 or be reminded here of how it is done. Turn the work inside out, as before, and then cast on the first shoulder seam with the outside (right side) of the garment facing you, then place the second shoulder seam on to the same needles with the inside (wrong side) facing you.
Cast off the pairs of stitches together, remembering to wind the yarn around each needle spike each time so that the casting off is even and not too tight. You should theoretically have pressed the edges of both pieces of the garment as each was completed; once you have done this, pin the side and sleeve seams. At the top of the slits on the side seams, cross over the hem edges neatly.

Now sit yourself down in front of the television and sew up your sweater dress. This should be therapeutic after the intense concentration of the past hours. If you have any doubts as to how to assemble the pieces, refer back to page 15 in chapter 1: it really is worth taking time and trouble at this stage, especially having got this far! There are several other techniques connected with weaving that you might like to explore at a later stage. I shall be touching on these on Sunday (see pages 87-89). Now you should have a well-earned rest, so sit back and enjoy your new dress. One thing I can safely guarantee: you will be feeling very pleased with yourself – and you will be wearing a garment that is utterly unique. What more could you ask of the day?

Thursday

You are now very nearly half-way through your knitting week. While Monday was designed to boost your confidence, Tuesday was a day of restraint; and on Wednesday you were able not only to express self-assurance in your knitting ability but also display the flamboyant side of your nature. Today, however, you can afford to take your confidence for granted. Thursday is therefore going to be a thoroughly professional day. You will be displaying full control of the situation and even the colours I propose you use are strictly economical: black and white, with perhaps just a hint of grey. The clarity of these lend themselves particularly well to the use of flat geometric patterns and it is these with which you will be experimenting in this chapter. As for the end garment incorporating these techniques, I suggest a crisp dress based on the same design as that employed on Wednesday. The result will be of great contrast and so should demonstrate most effectively how the same design can be used for two totally different looks, both in terms of colour, the visual and tactile quality of the knitted fabric and the mood they create. Before choosing the yarns for your first 'Jacquard', put away all the confusion of colours used yesterday; you will now find it much easier to concentrate on your black and off-white yarns. For the first few swatches, I suggest you stick to one black 3-ply wool yarn and one in an off-white: unless the yarn is really superb, bright white, when used with black, can look a little harsh.

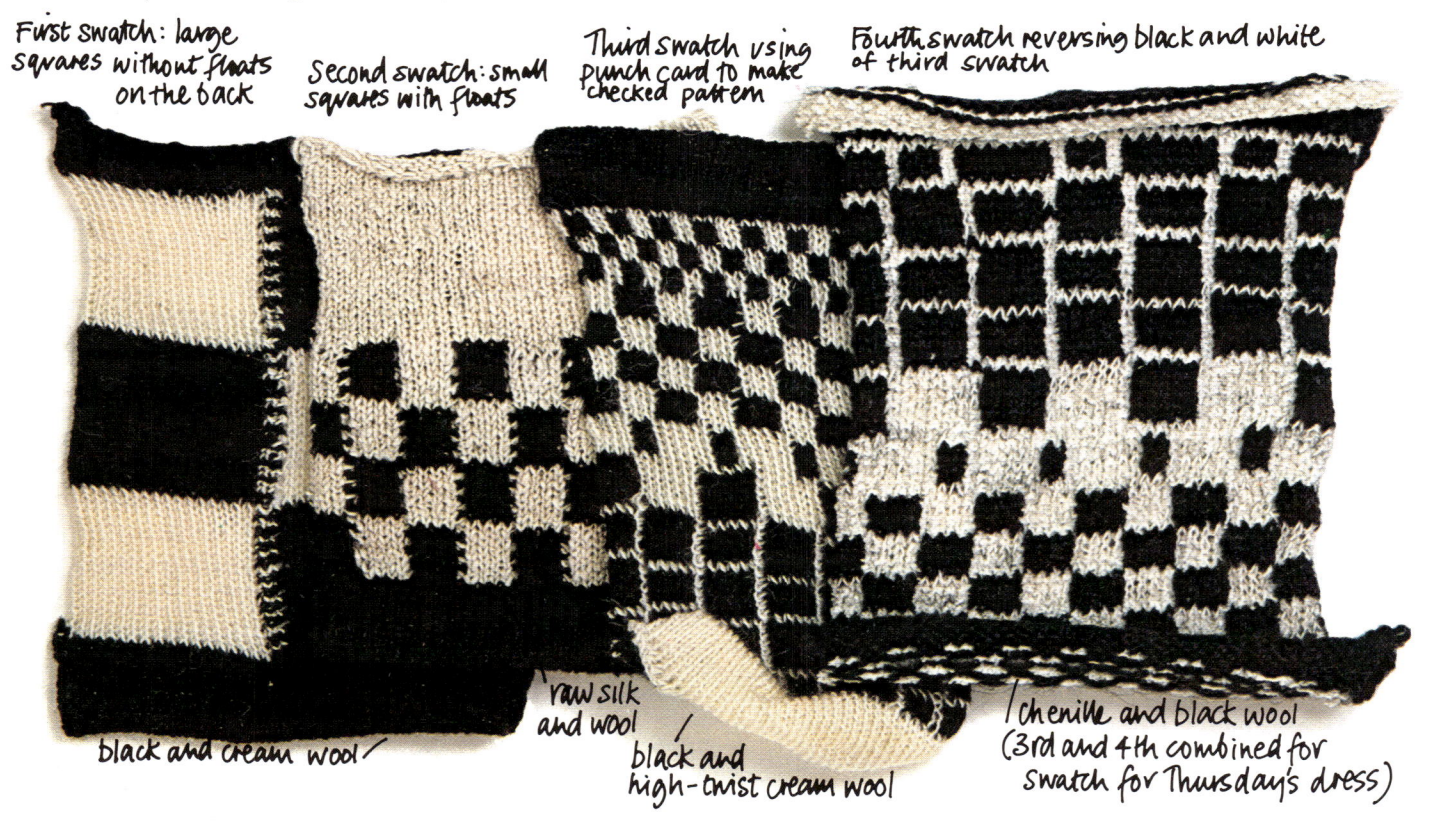

First swatch: large squares without floats on the back

Second swatch: small squares with floats

Third swatch using punch card to make checked pattern

Fourth swatch reversing black and white of third swatch

black and cream wool

raw silk and wool

black and high-twist cream wool

chenille and black wool (3rd and 4th combined for swatch for Thursday's dress)

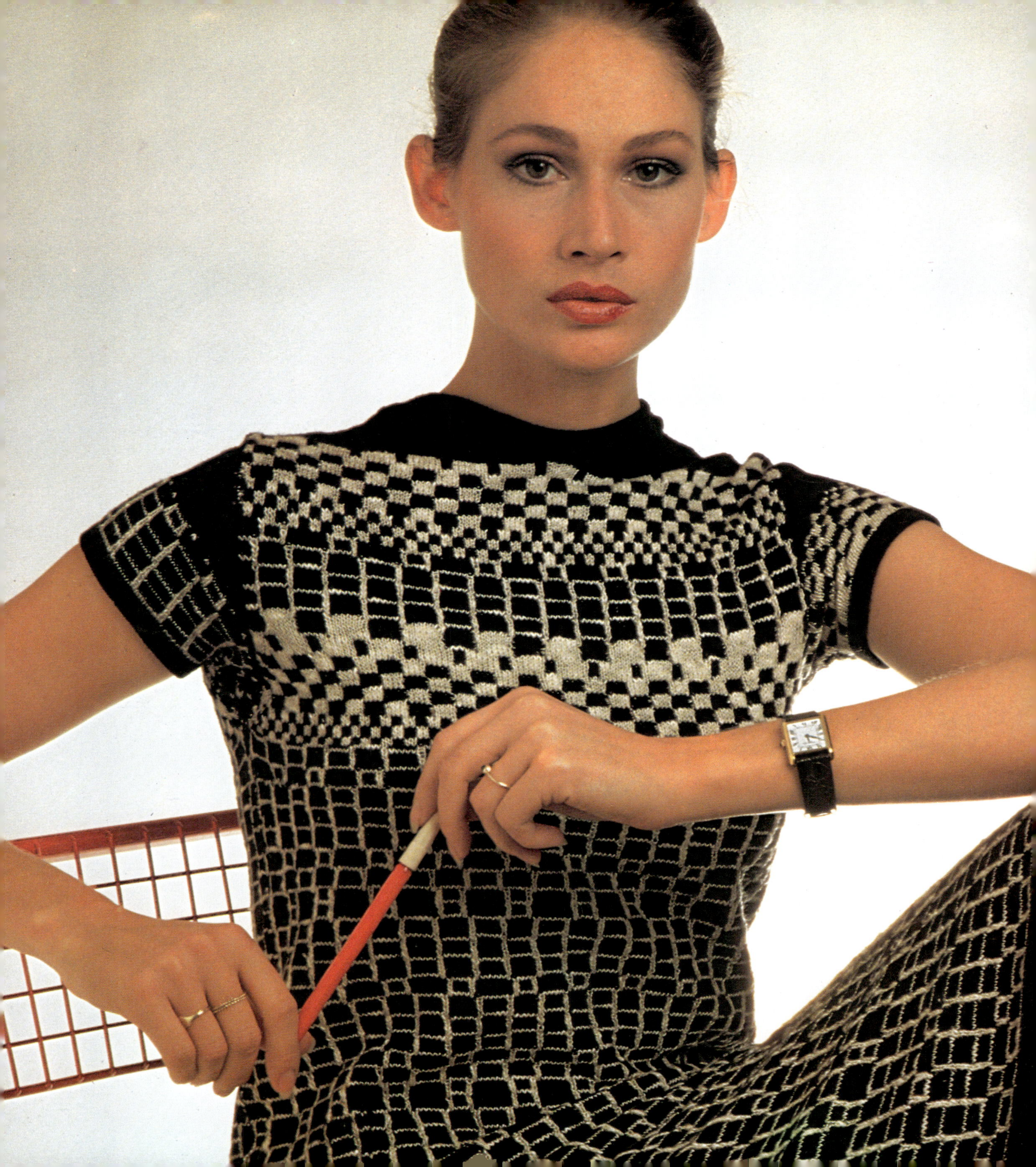

Diagram 1
With the machine threaded and the off-white yarn out of the way, cast on using black and knit several rows at a tension suitable for the selected yarn. Hang weights on the knitting.
Divide the number of needles on which you are knitting into two, pushing the half furthest away from the carriage out of action. Programme your machine to knit only those needles in the knitting position and knit two rows (a).
Now push out all the needles, remove the yarn from the carriage and hook it out of the way, then take the empty carriage across to the other side of the swatch (b). Once in this position, push into knitting position all the needles that you have not yet knitted, including the two most central needles. Knit two more rows. Remove the yarn, push out all the needles and bring the empty carriage back across to where you first began.
Push the first half of the needles into knitting position, together with the first needle from the other half of the needles. By using these two central needles, the yarns will twist around each other and so prevent a hole forming down the dividing line between the black and white yarns (c). Repeat this operation until two squares – one black and one white – have built up on your swatch. Once you have knitted enough rows for regular squares (make a note of the number!), it is time to change the colours so that the next two squares are in reverse: instead of knitting the next two rows in black, you will knit them in off-white, and so on. This will create a checked effect.

Diagram 2
To do this, cut the black yarn, remove it from the carriage and substitute with off-white yarn. This means that where you were knitting with black you will now be using off-white, and where you were knitting with off-white you will

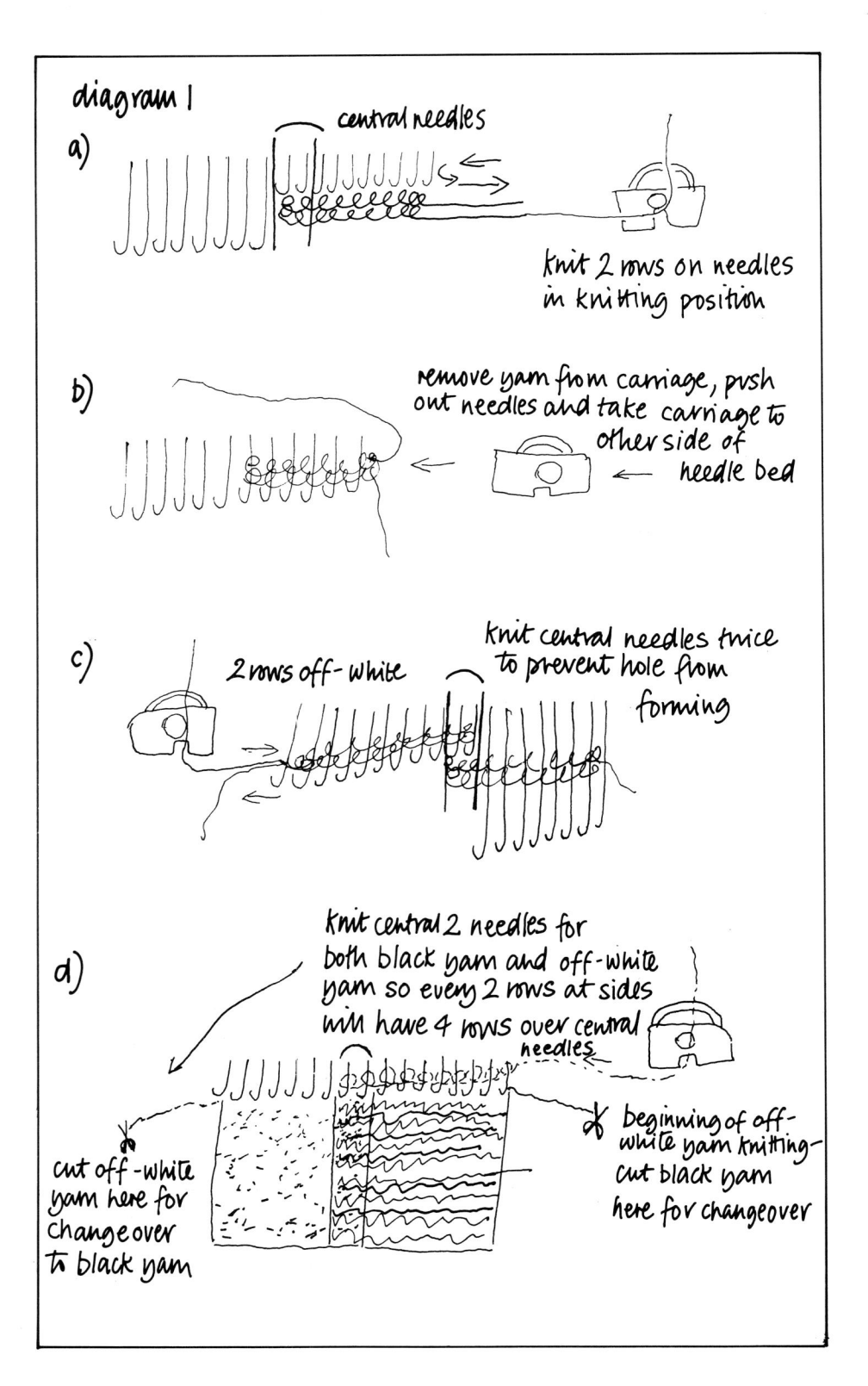

be using black. Continue knitting to form two more squares.

Diagram 3
Vary the pattern now in any one of three or more ways. Either knit in stripes (a) or one colour only (b) or allow small holes to form down the central line that divides the two halves of the swatch (c). You can do this by knitting over the two central needles every two rows rather than every one row. Alternatively, by not knitting the central needles twice on every row you can create longer slits (d). However, unless these are to be part of your intended design, it would be quicker to knit each square separately and then join them together afterwards.

Diagram 4
There is another method of knitting squares for a checked pattern that also does not resort to using punch cards. Though not quite as time consuming as the technique just described, it is still relatively slow and therefore cannot be recommended for an entire garment. For details and small areas, such as borders, it can be most effective however.
Unlike the first technique (a), this method creates 'floats' on the back (or the front if this is what is intended) of the knitting (b). If you carry a yarn from one place where you have been using it to another position in the pattern, the length not knitted in will 'float' on the surface from one set of needles to another.
One final point: if you make the size of the squares for your checks too large, you will find ears, earrings and rings getting caught in the floats of the finished garment. Just bear this in mind when you design your fabric.

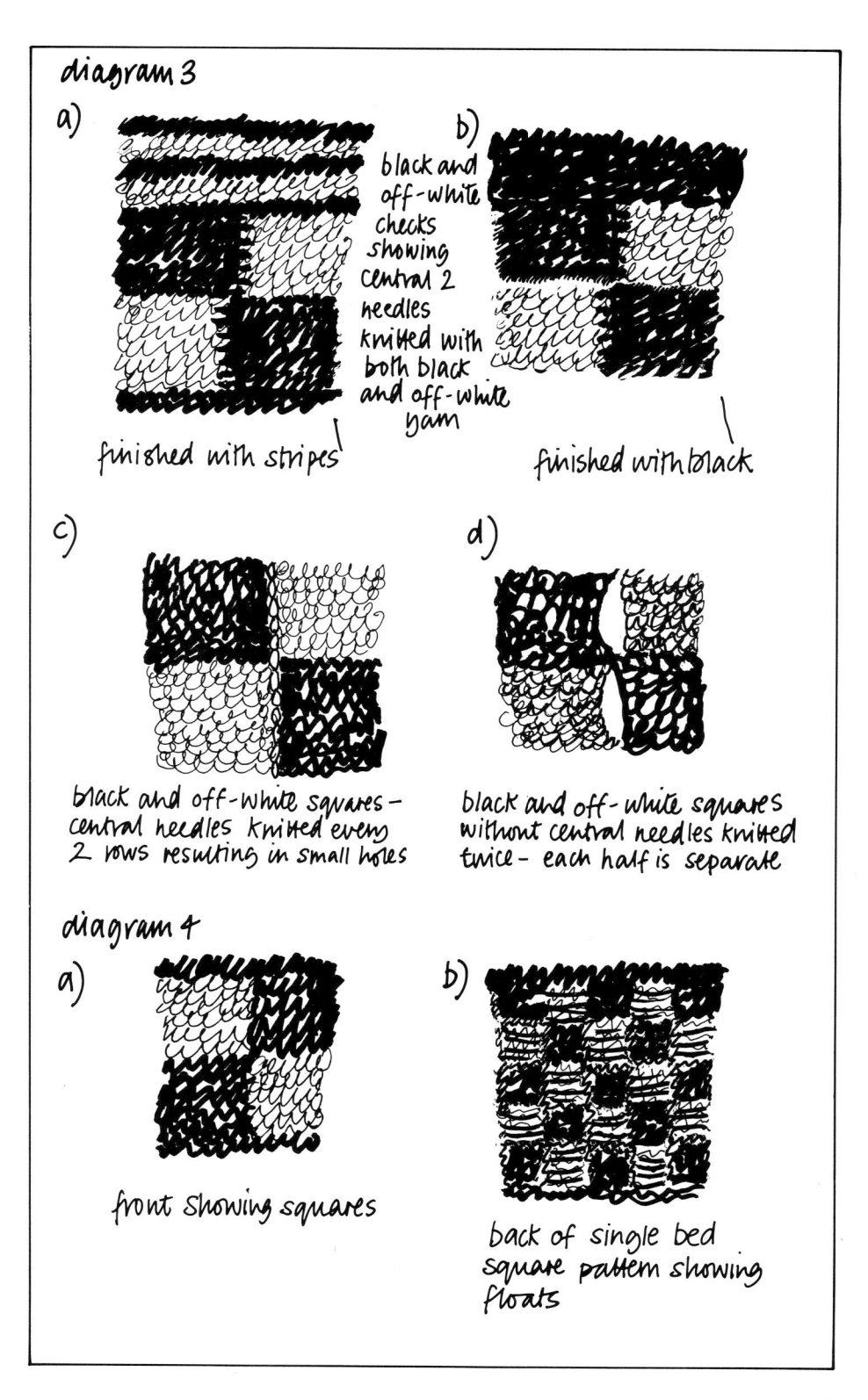

diagram 3

a) finished with stripes

b) black and off-white checks showing central 2 needles knitted with both black and off-white yarn — finished with black

c) black and off-white squares – central needles knitted every 2 rows resulting in small holes

d) black and off-white squares without central needles knitted twice – each half is separate

diagram 4

a) front showing squares

b) back of single bed square pattern showing floats

Diagram 5
It is time now to knit your second swatch. Cast on to a suitable number of needles and knit several rows using the same yarn and tension as before. Decide how large you want the squares to be for this smaller chequerboard pattern – between three and six needles would be about right; I shall compromise with four. Push out groups of four needles (a) and then check that the machine will knit only those needles in the knitting position. Knit two rows. Pull back the needles that were out of action without any of the stitches falling off and then, while holding the knitting on to the machine, pull out all the other needles (b). Assuming that you did not drop any of the stitches, change over the yarns from black to off-white and knit two rows. Bring out the original sets of needles and change the yarn (c). Knit two rows. Continue knitting until you have a row of black and white squares.

Diagram 6
If you want regular checks, change the needles and yarns at regular intervals over a set number of rows (a); for irregular checks, change the yarns and needles at irregular intervals over an irregular number of rows (b).

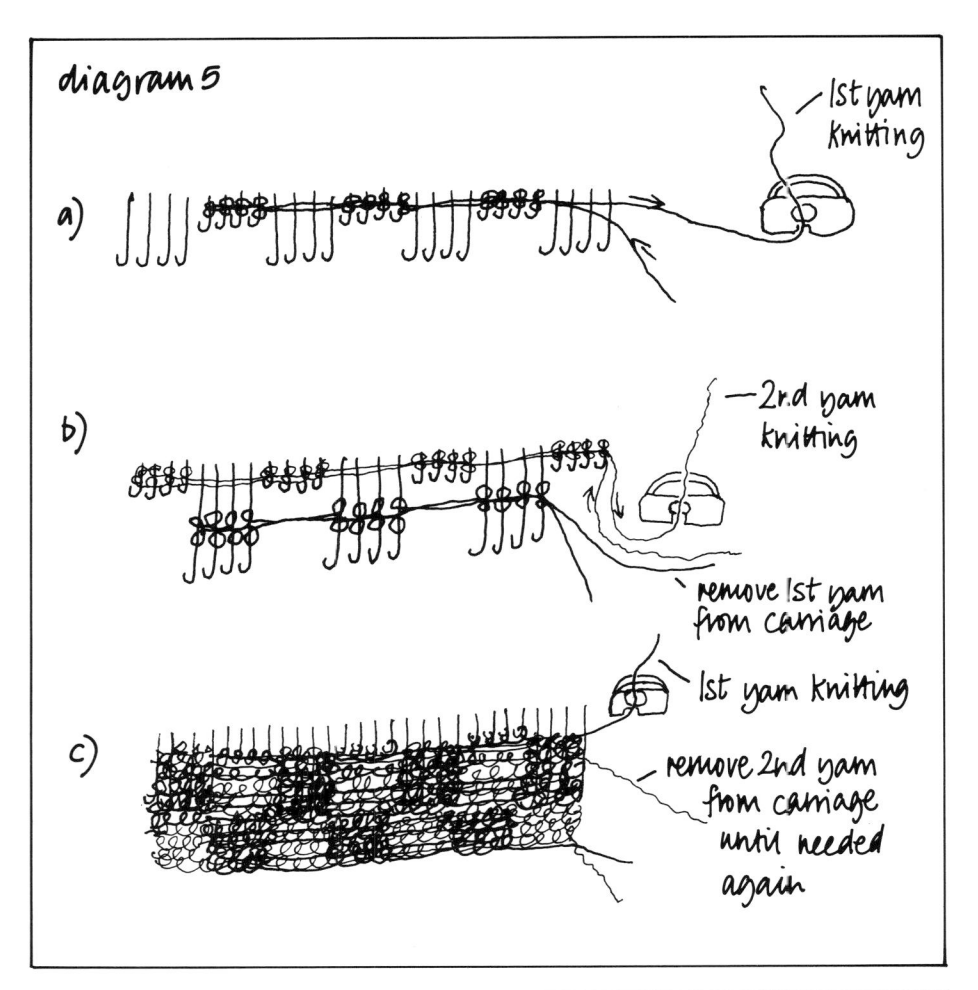

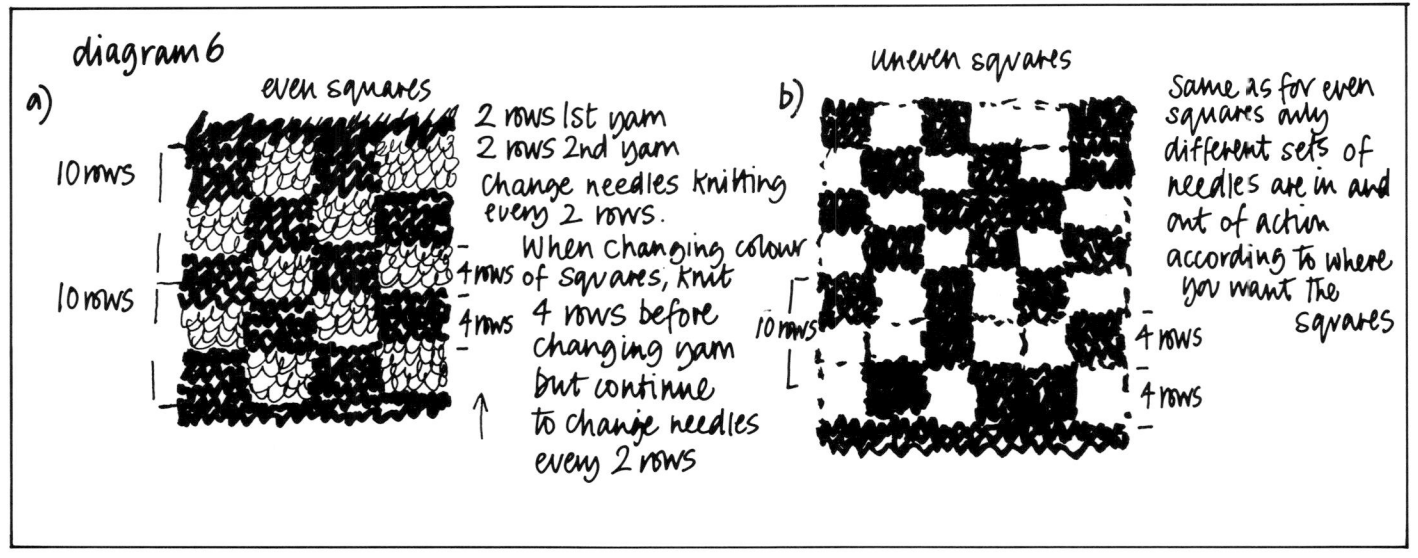

diagram 7
for a regular square you usually need more rows to the centimetre or inch than stitches

5 rows
4 stitches

diagram 8

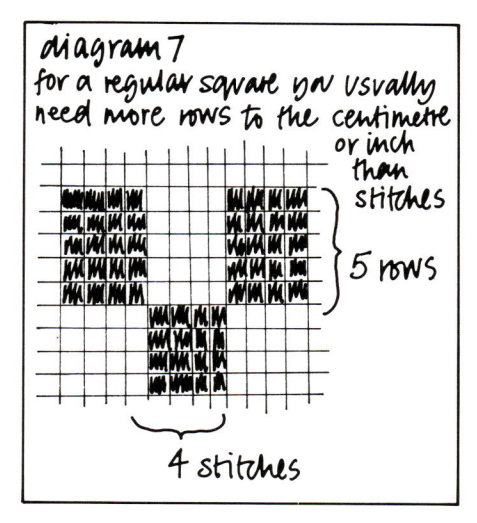

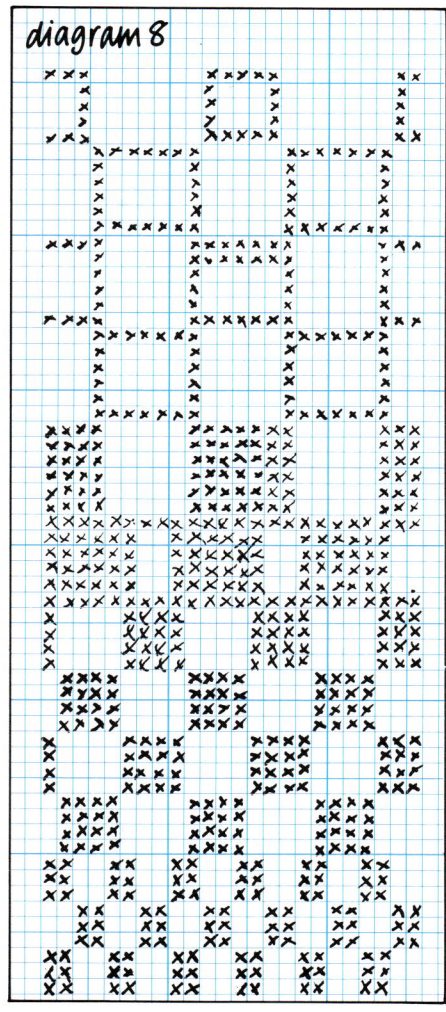

Diagram 7
Both the techniques you have just put into practice can be operated on any single bed machine. For more complicated patterns charted on graph paper, your machine will require either a simple 'Fair Isle' programmer, a punch card system, or needles of such a large gauge that it will not take forever pushing them in and out.

Diagram 8
In knitting a square of equal sides, you should by now have realised that there are usually more rows to every 2.5cm (1 in) than there are stitches to the same measure. You have to take this into account, of course, when working out a pattern on graph paper. For example, for a check four stitches wide, you will probably have to knit about five rows in order to create a regular square.

In order to count accurately so that you can chart your pattern on graph paper, knit a plain tension swatch using one of the yarns you intend using in your design.

perfect squares
A

badly marked out squares
B

B
A

A taking into account that there are more rows than stitches
B not taking into account that there are more rows per centimetre or inch than there are stitches

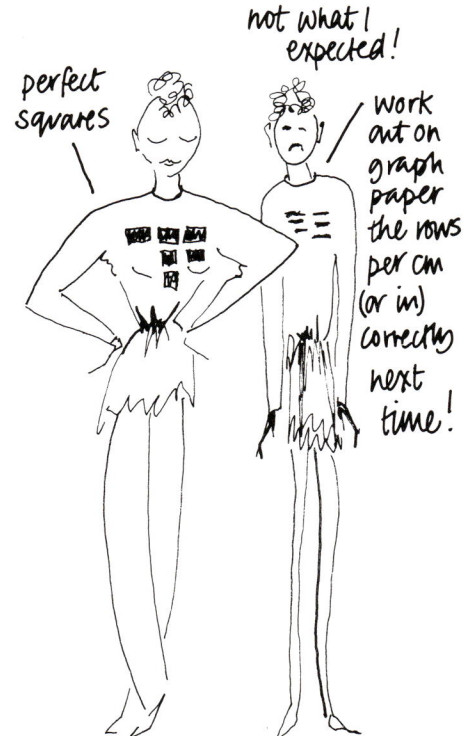

perfect squares

not what I expected!
work out on graph paper the rows per cm (or in) correctly next time!

Diagram 9
Depending on the make of your machine, either work directly from graph paper on to the machine itself, or, even more conveniently, punch out your pattern on a card and insert this into the machine. This facility means that you will have little else to think about until you reach the end of your knitting.

But what if your machine is not this sophisticated? You will probably have push down buttons instead; they control the needles that are to be knitted or not and are easy to use, but obviously the whole operation will be much more mechanical.

Whatever type of machine you have, refer to your manual to see exactly how to use it for this type of pattern; since I usually knit with one that has a punch card system, this is the method I shall explain for making today's dress. Punch cards can be purchased at most department stores that stock knitting machines; the punch – a tool that creates the holes that dictate the pattern – is usually sold as an accessory with the machine itself.

Diagram 10
Refer back to the graph pattern shown in diagram 8 and note that it falls into two natural sections: one in which the black predominates and the other that appears mainly white.
Begin by making several swatches.

Diagram 11
For the first, try using black yarn threaded through the first yarn feed. After casting on, knit several rows in black and then thread the off-white through the second yarn feed. Turn the punch card to the beginning of the pattern, set the machine to knit Fair Isle and check that the carriage is programmed to knit the needles in all positions. To ensure you are at the beginning of the pattern, turn the card several times and check the pattern panel: if it shows all the teeth, you are in the right place to start.

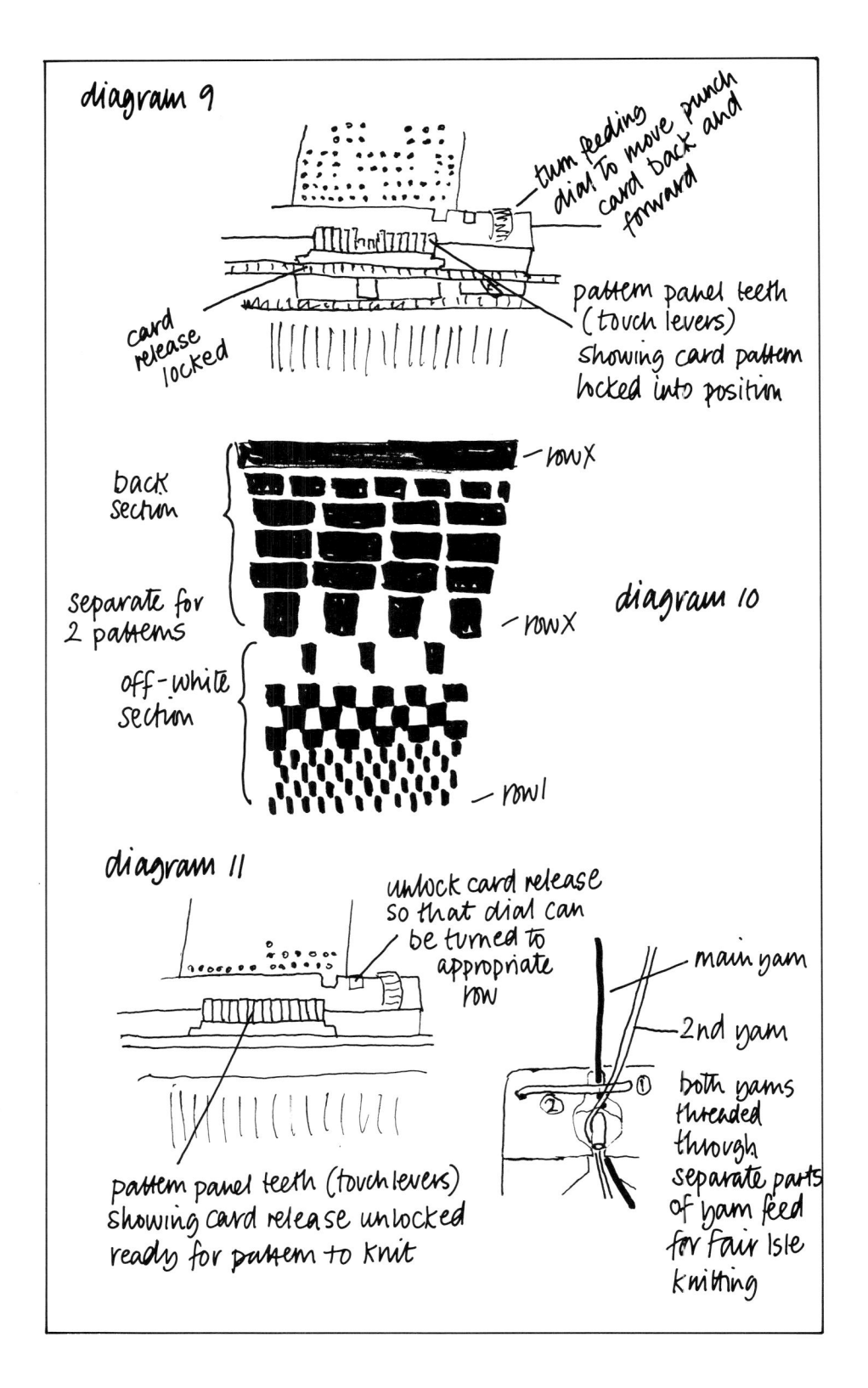

56

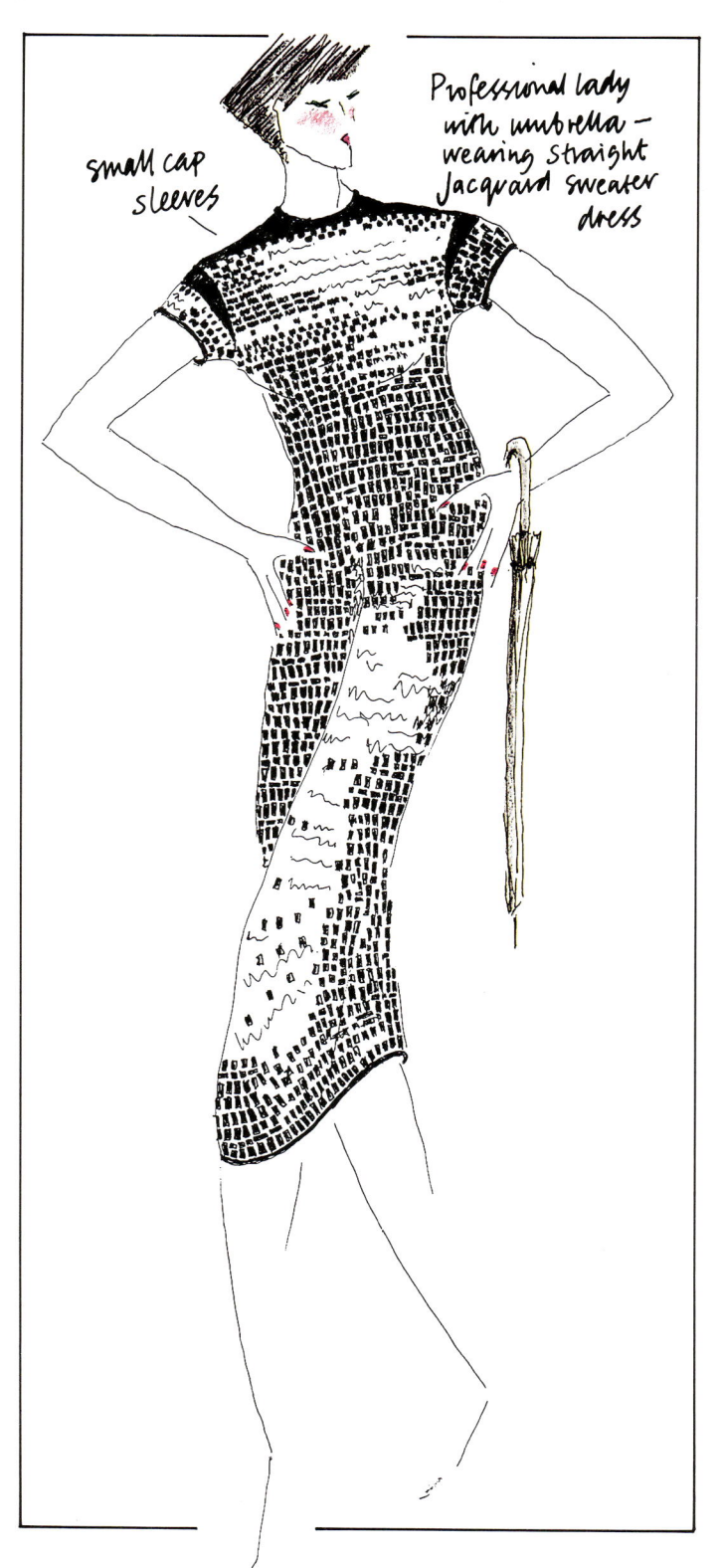

small cap sleeves

Professional lady with umbrella — wearing straight Jacquard sweater dress

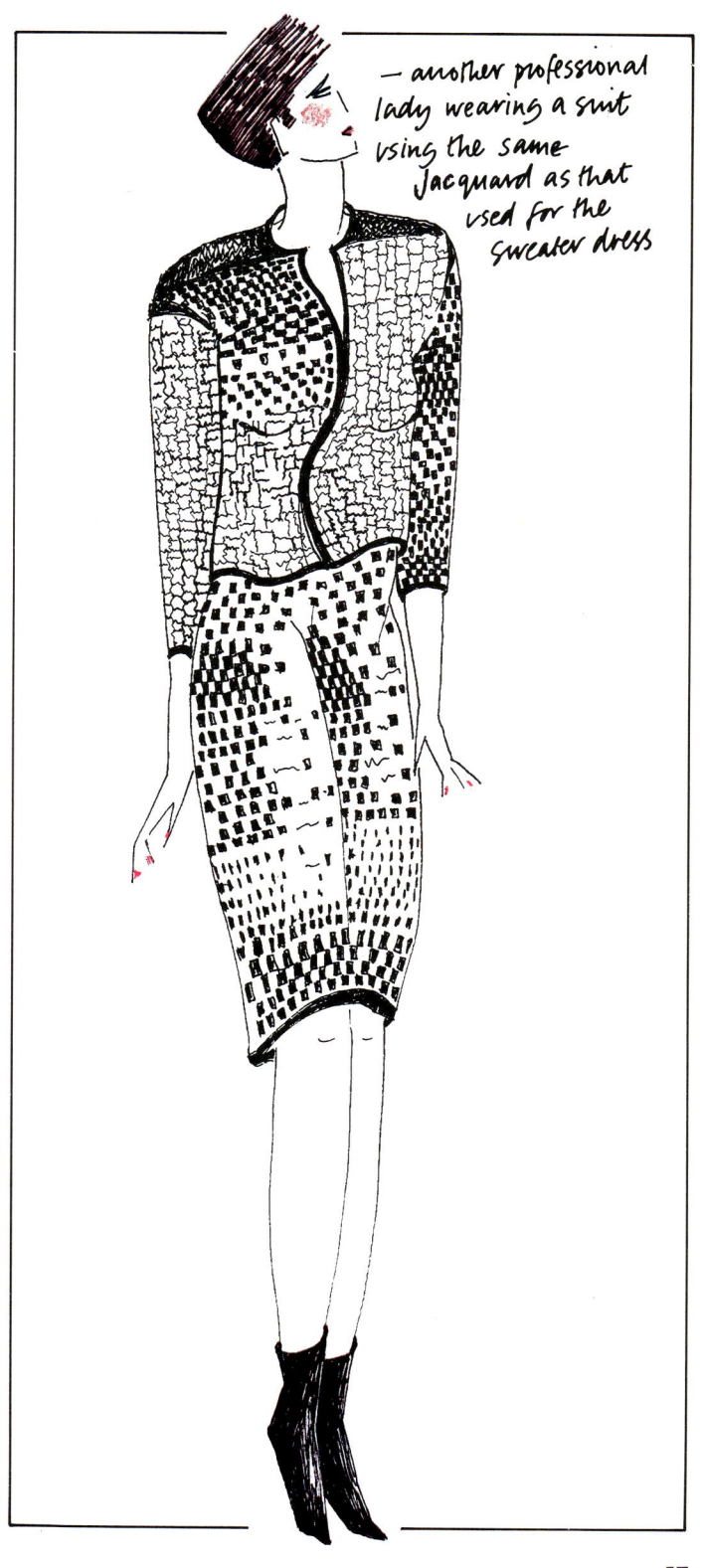

— another professional lady wearing a suit using the same Jacquard as that used for the sweater dress

Diagram 12

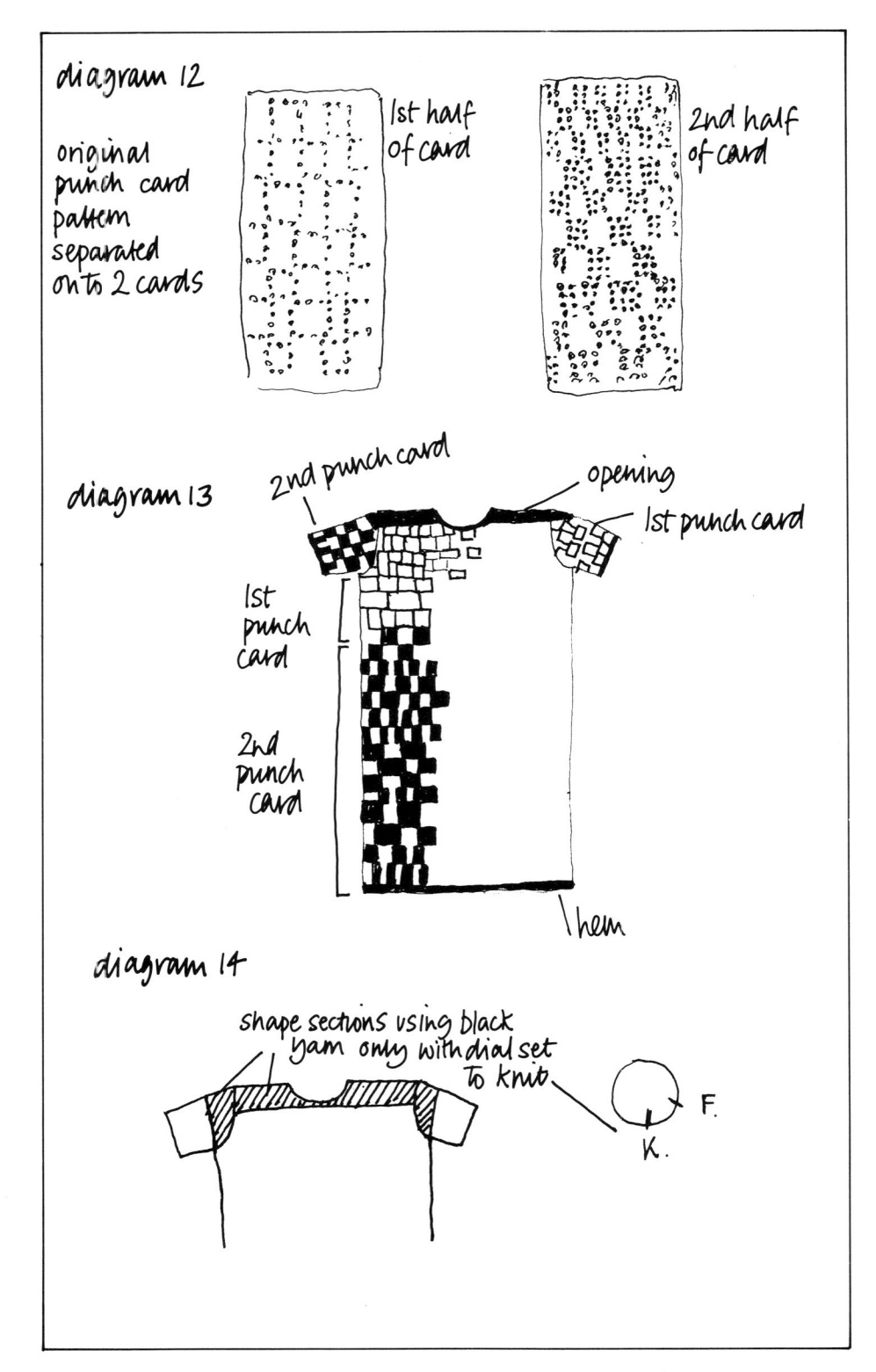

Before starting the pattern, turn your row counter to zero and when you reach the blacker area of the design, note the number of rows you have just knitted. Also record the number of rows in the second section of the design. If you know the number of rows for each part, you can use the patterns separately without punching out two cards. If you find it easier to use two separate cards, however, punch out each separate section of the design, repeating it until the punch-card is completely covered. If the pattern does not repeat exactly, you can always improvise a little.

Once you have completed this first swatch – and this includes pressing it according to the yarns suitability – knit another. This time, thread the off-white yarn through the first yarn feed and the black through the second. Compare the two swatches and see how the patterns are reversed.

Now try other swatches using different off-white yarns: chenille, cotton, fluffy yarns, slubbed wools and any others you think may look good together. Remember though! They *must* all be of the same weight.

When you finally have two swatches that incorporate the yarns you want to use, one predominantly in black and the other mostly white, you are ready to cast on for the dress itself.

Diagram 13

Having estimated the number of stitches and rows per 2.5cm (1 in) you can begin working from the same basic dress design as that followed on Wednesday. The shape will be virtually identical so make a scale drawing and fill it in with the geometric pattern you intend to follow. The only parts that will not be patterned will be those areas where there are needles out of action – the shaping of the neck and sleeve heads. The hems around the bottom, on the neck and sleeves, will also be plain.

Diagram 14
For these sections, turn the dial so that you can knit in one colour only and, where necessary, programme the machine to knit only those needles that you have in the knitting position.

Diagram 15
There are several variations you can incorporate into Wednesday's design to make the style of today's dress just a bit different, such as shortening the sleeves. Instead of leaving an opening down the back, place it along one shoulder; knit two small hems to overlap the edges and then sew on poppers to close the opening.
Apart from these changes, you should have little problem in making this garment, so long as you keep in mind the possibility that because your tension is more than likely to be different, when you come to shape the neck, armholes and sleeve heads you may have to decrease over more or fewer stitches and rows. By now, however, you should be able to cope with this.
Once the dress is finished, try it on. How different it looks from Wednesday's style! The combination of yarns, design and pattern and the colourway you used should all convey a look that makes you feel thoroughly competent and professional – if you have got this far, you have proved that you are!
Now you can use a basic pattern to make any number of dresses, each reflecting a completely different mood and designed to suit a variety of occasions and situations.
Once you are confident that you can make a dress with a shaped neckline like this, it is an easy enough matter to make a matching cardigan. If the prospect of making pockets or buttonholes is too tiresome or daunting, fasten with a brooch or a few of Monday's rouleaux. Obviously, you will not have time to do this today but it is well worth keeping in mind for a future project.

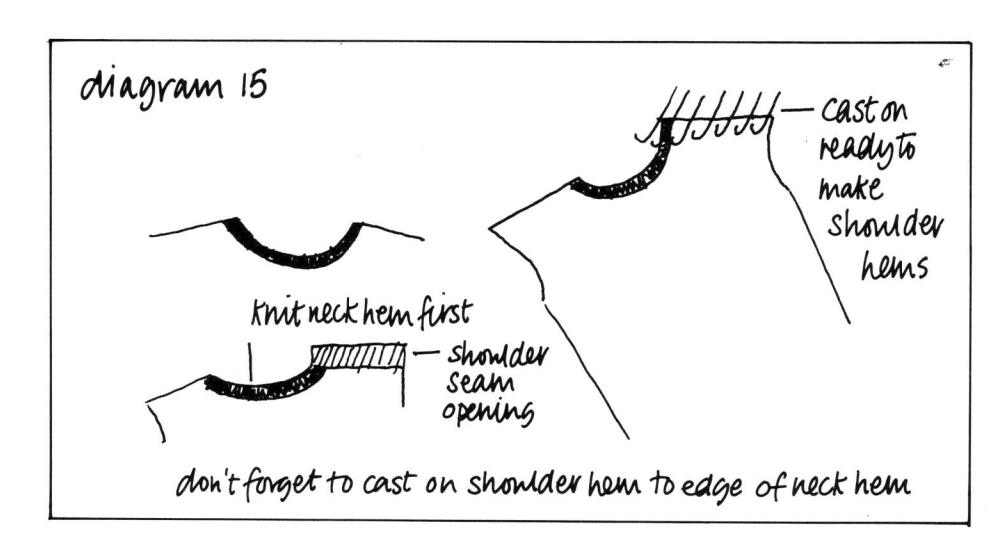

diagram 15 — knit neck hem first — shoulder seam opening — cast on ready to make shoulder hems
don't forget to cast on shoulder hem to edge of neck hem

Now you are definitely over half-way through the week, and already you are the proud owner – and designer – of a bandeau, a jersey and two dresses. It seems logical to think next in terms of making a garment to cover them all. Tomorrow, then, a jacket?

Now what I really need is a KNITTED JACKET!

Friday

So far this week, you have concentrated on making garments that can be worn on their own; today I propose that you create something to wear either over some of the knitted shapes you have already made or which would prove useful over the rest of your non-knitted clothes. A jacket certainly seems a good idea, being a classical addition to any wardrobe. Since the garment I have in mind is essentially simple in line, practical and designed not to date, I suggest you use yarns that are primarily tweedy and earthy in both texture and colour, with accents of grey-blue or green chenille and mohair.

Test the elasticity of the various yarns you have selected and make swatches of each. The more elastic the yarn, the more suitable it will prove to be for the new technique you are about to learn and explore: tucking. I think it only fair to warn you that chenille (the yarn that I shall be using) is very inelastic and so not easy to use; so choose another yarn if you find it too troublesome.

With the project and yarns thus settled, it is time to explore the potential of tuck stitch. So far, all the textured effects you have achieved are the result of changing the tension of the machine in combination with the use of different textured yarns, or by weaving by hand and machine.

For tucking, the stitches are held on selected needles which gather to produce a tuck. One row is then knitted on the collected stitches before returning to tucking again.

First swatch showing random blisters made by pushing out needles

Second swatch making blisters in same way as first but regularly

(–both 3rd and 4th swatch knitted on alternate needles)

Third swatch using punch card for tucking and making blisters

Fourth swatch with chenille stripes used as tension swatch

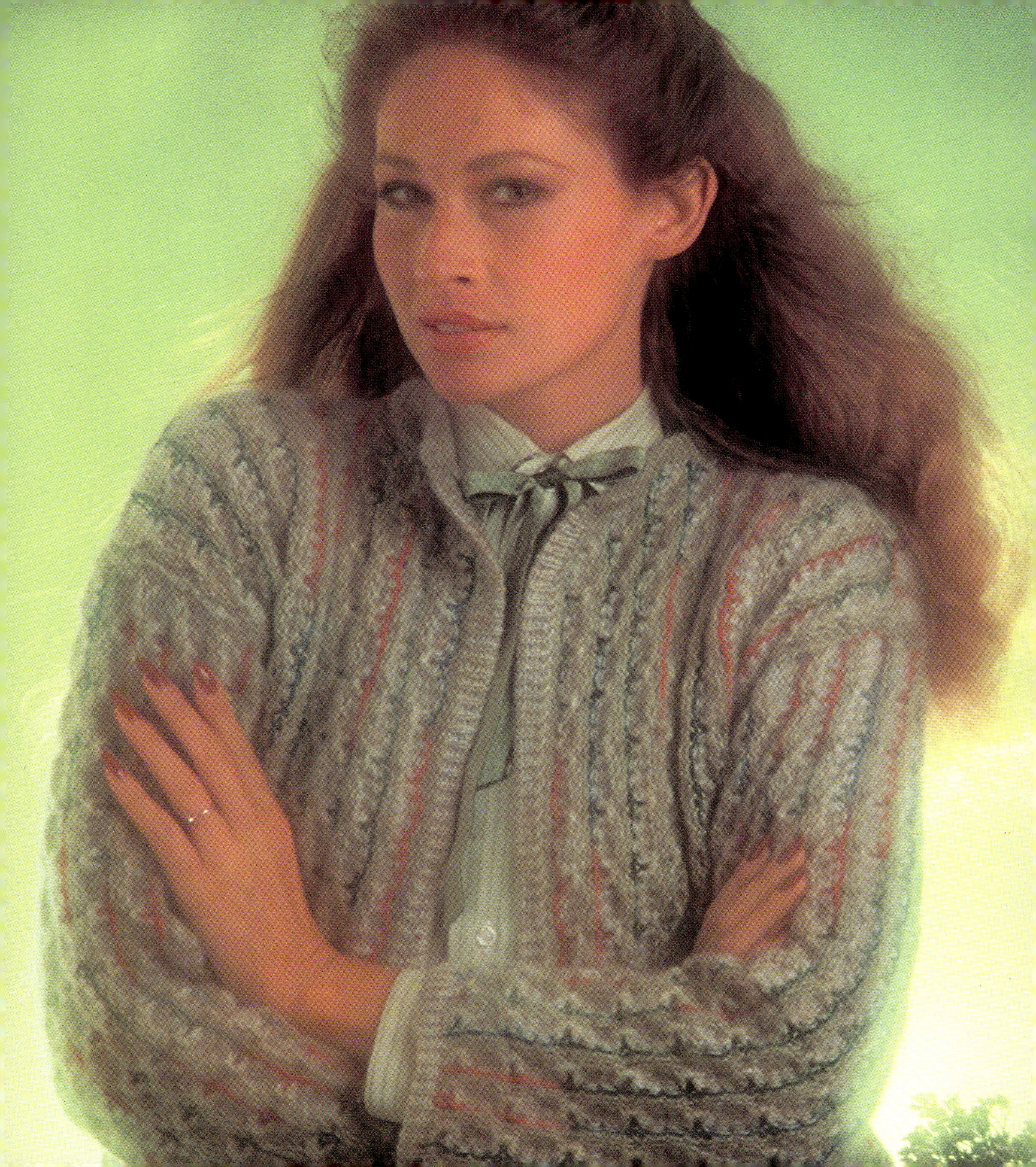

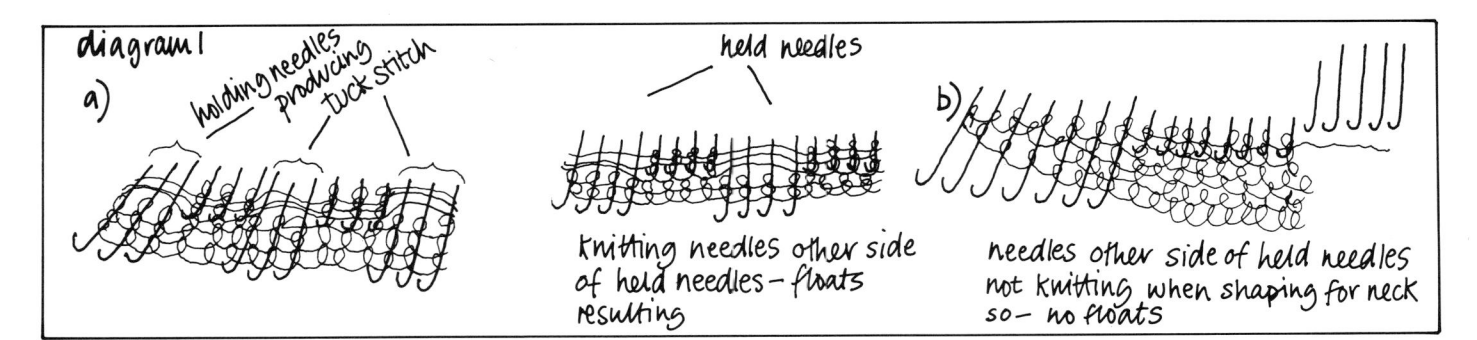

Diagram 1 (a) holding needles producing tuck stitch

held needles

knitting needles other side of held needles - floats resulting

b) needles other side of held needles not knitting when shaping for neck so - no floats

Diagram 1
Tuck stitch is the result of holding needles (a), a technique that you have already practised. Do you remember holding needles when shaping the neck for Wednesday's and Thursday's projects? In each of those situations, you avoided creating floats by not knitting beyond the needles being held (b).
Just as you explored the Jacquard designs on Thursday's swatches, it is possible to tuck either with or without punch cards. Begin today's first sample without using one.
Although tucking with the use of a punch card is quicker, by selecting needles by hand, you will be able to design your tuck pattern as you knit, varying the shapes of the tucks so that they appear either as very large 'blisters', or tiny ones.

Diagram 2
Before casting on for your first swatch, choose a blueish tweedy yarn for the background and possibly a grey-blue chenille, fine wool or any other yarn that proves appropriate to the technique for the tucked blisters. Gather other suitable yarns around you so that you can change the background colour half-way through the swatch should you so choose, making sure that you are quite happy they all work together.
Cast on at a suitable tension with the background yarn, knit several rows and secure weights in position. Now change to the chenille yarn, fine wool or whatever and programme the

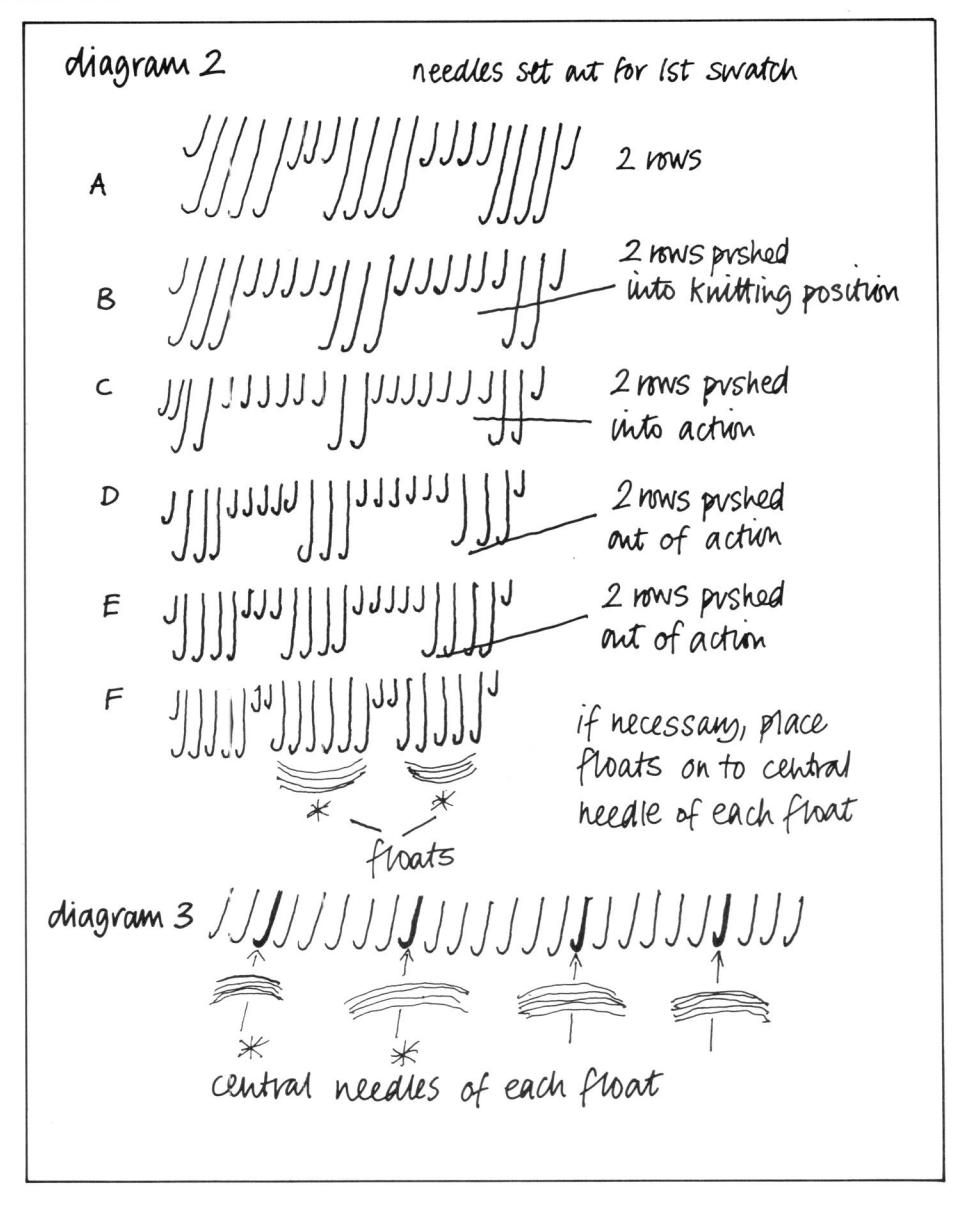

diagram 2 needles set out for 1st swatch

A — 2 rows
B — 2 rows pushed into knitting position
C — 2 rows pushed into action
D — 2 rows pushed out of action
E — 2 rows pushed out of action
F — if necessary, place floats on to central needle of each float

floats

diagram 3 central needles of each float

62

carriage to knit only those needles in action. Push out the needles as shown in A, knit two rows, bring needles (B) into knitting position, knit two rows, bring needles (C) into knitting position, knit two rows. Rows D-F require you to follow the same procedure in reverse. Instead of pushing needles into position and knitting two rows, push them gradually out of action and then knit two rows.

Diagram 3
After row F in the previous diagram, change back to the main background yarn, knit two rows, and then, if you are in any way worried about the floats, or wish to use them as part of your design, bring out the needle central to each float, hook the floats over each of these needles and then knit two rows.

Diagram 4
Now you have a choice. You can either knit more rows in your basic yarn before changing to chenille or another suitable yarn for blisters, or you change to this second yarn after only two rows. Try knitting about eight rows before making the next series of blisters, placing them as shown (a). This means that you will be knitting tucks only on those needles in dark areas as in the diagram. Use the same principle to knit the blisters as used in diagram 2 but follow the pattern given (b). Once you have completed this swatch, cast off and steam it by holding the iron above the fabric; pressing will only flatten the blisters and spoil the very effect you are trying to achieve. Creating tucks by hand is a time consuming exercise as you will now have discovered. For this reason, space them out; they are far more effective used like this in a design anyway.

Diagram 5
It can be helpful to make a quick sketch of a proposed swatch just as I have done, marking the position of the proposed blisters.

Once you have mastered the basic tucking technique, experiment with a few more swatches, changing your background yarns and substituting the chenille or the yarn you are using with something equally interesting. Hopefully you will soon have a collection of beautifully blistered swatches. You have? Good.

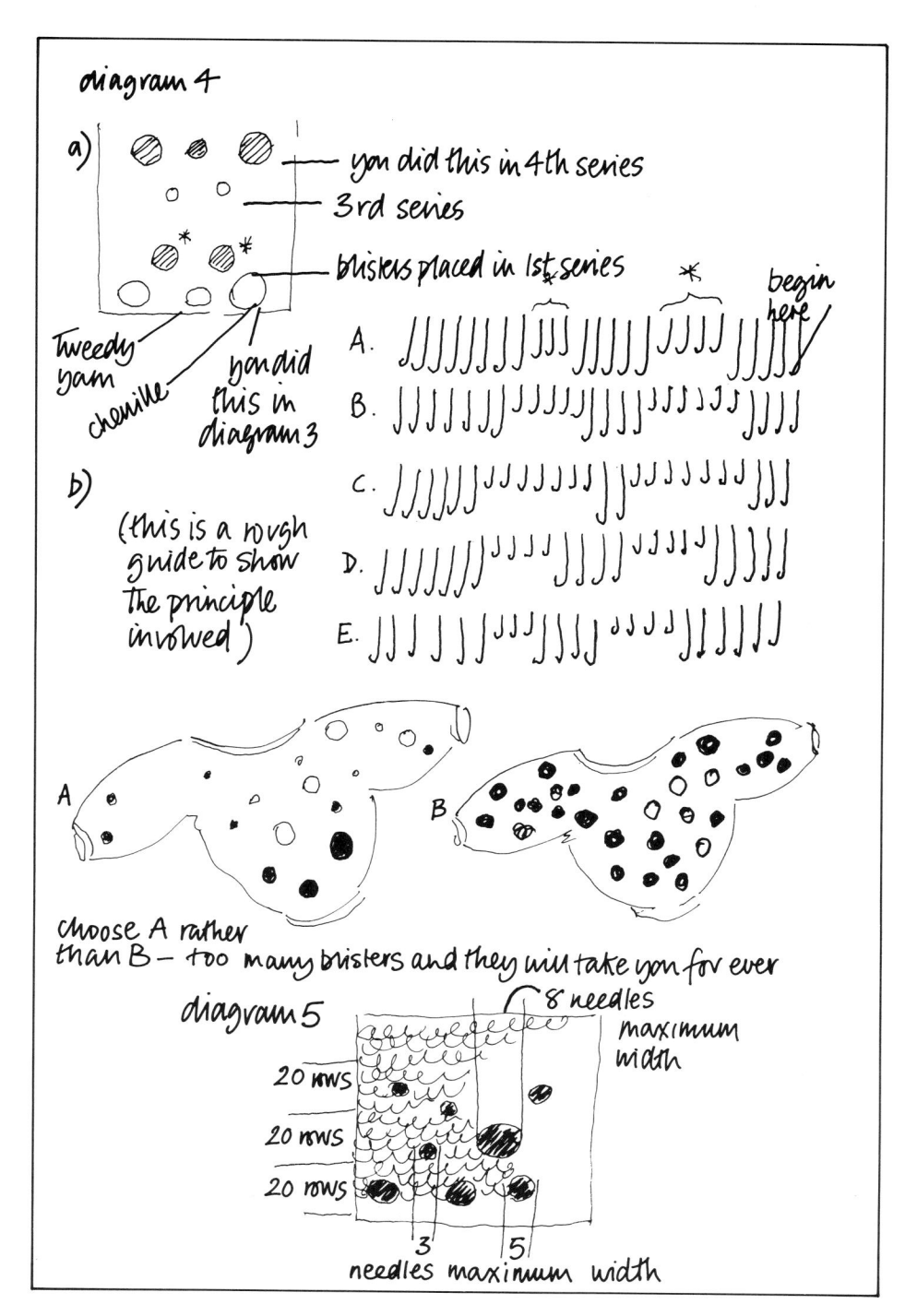

diagram 6

needles 2, 5, 8 will tuck for as many rows as you have your carriage programmed to tuck

needles selected to tuck

needle selection panel

Once you reprogramme the machine to knit, all needles you have been tucking will knit

diagram 7

Section of a punch card showing which needles will hold and which will knit

needles knitting
held needles
locked position of pattern

diagram 8

tuck position for carriage to tuck stitch punch card

knit position on carriage for most machines

carriage side levers either on I or II depending on machine

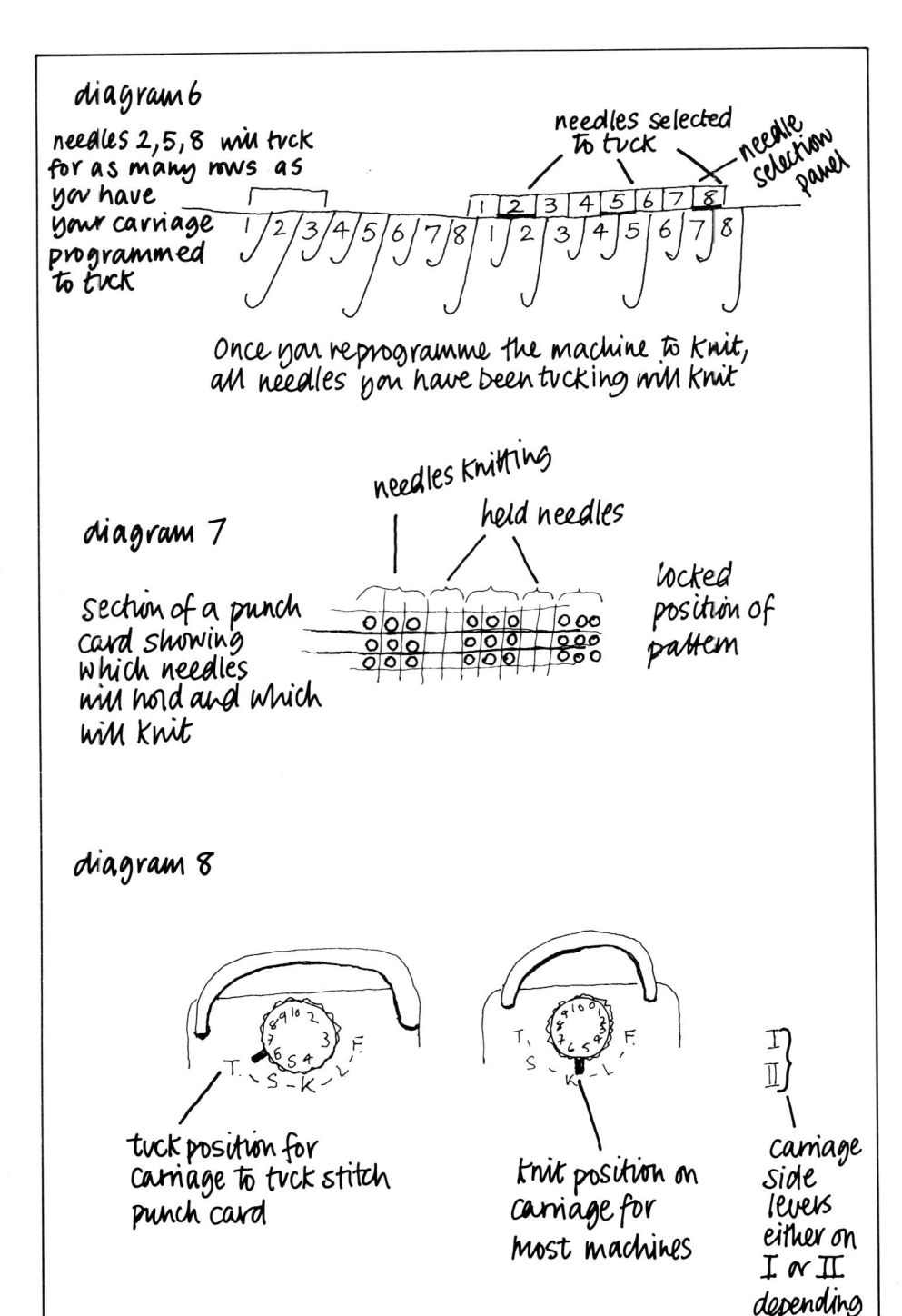

Diagram 6
For the second series of swatches, use punch cards to tuck the fabric. If your machine does not have them it probably uses a method of needle selection similar to that described on Thursday for knitting a flat pattern. However, in order to make tucks rather than a flat pattern, make sure your machine is programmed to knit tucks and not Fair Isle.

Diagram 7
Assuming your machine has a punch card system as does mine, it should also have a pack of punch cards. If it does not you will have to punch your own as you did for the Fair Isle pattern on Thursday. So why not use that one; once you understand the principle of punch card tucking, you can either make your own or use those that are supplied with your machine. For the moment however, use a portion of the card you punched out yesterday.

Diagram 8
The holes that are punched are always knitted; the solid squares create the pattern, the needles relating to the squares being held. With the machine programmed to tuck, and the punch card locked on to a specific row for the duration of the knitting, the needles that relate to the solid squares on the pattern will be held for every row knitted with the machine programmed to tuck. Once you have re-programmed the machine to ignore the punch card, so that it will knit rather than tuck, it should do exactly that.
Do you remember that on Tuesday you knitted your jumper on alternate needles? I think it would be a good idea to do the same thing here, as it will allow you to use a thicker yarn and thereby knit a thicker, warmer garment.

Friday's jacket belted

Friday's jacket open

...worn with grey cap, trousers and white shoes

space-dyed chenille and mohair

Diagram 9 (handwritten labels)

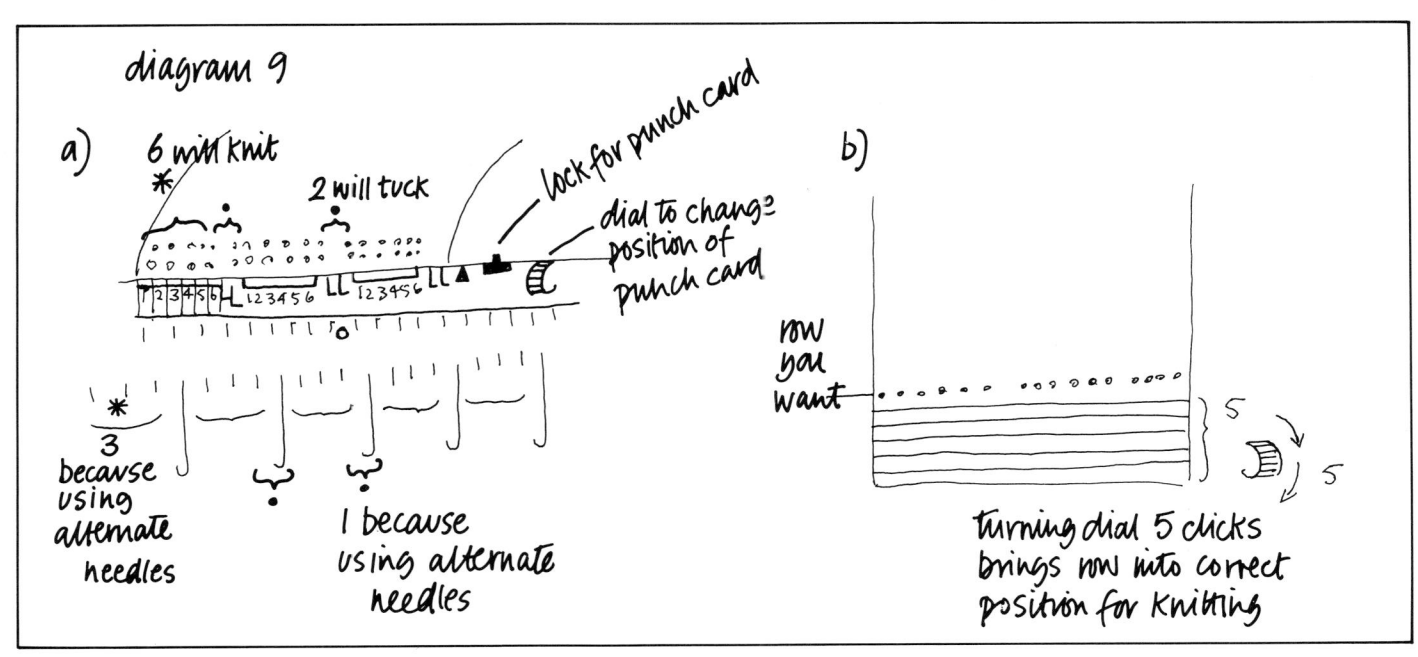

a) 6 will knit · 2 will tuck · lock for punch card · dial to change position of punch card · 3 because using alternate needles · 1 because using alternate needles

b) row you want · turning dial 5 clicks brings row into correct position for knitting

Diagram 10 (handwritten labels)

2nd yarn out of the way · 1st yarn through yarn feed · 3rd yarn on floor beside you

Diagram 9
Before you begin to knit the next swatch, make sure your punch card is set at the correct row. To do this, select the row you want to use, turn the card in its holder until the row you have chosen is visible above the holder and then turn the card five squares – or however many squares your machine demands according to your manual – towards you, so locking it into position (a and b).

Diagram 10
Choose three yarns: two should be contrasting tweedy yarns, the other a plain or space-dyed chenille or slub. Thread one of the two main yarns through the yarn feed and tie the second out of the way. Place the third more decorative yarn on the floor beside you. Cast on to 20 alternate needles for 20 stitches over 40 needles. Knit two rows, then secure the weights in the usual way. Change to the second main yarn, turn the stitch programme to 'tuck' and knit six rows. Remove the 'tucking' yarn, replace it with the 'knitting' yarn and knit one row. Remove the yarn from the yarn feed.

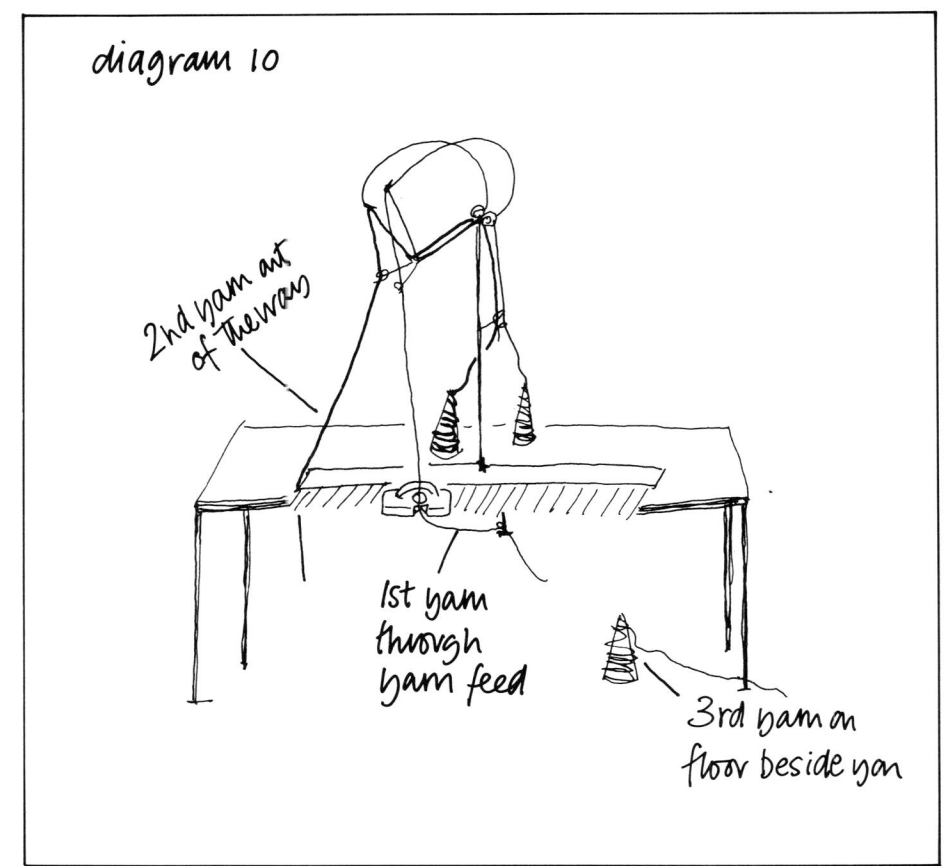

Diagram 11
Thread the end of the chenille or whatever yarn you have used as a substitute yarn through the yarn feed. Secure it in place and then, holding the yarn as it is drawn from the cone above the carriage, knit one row (a and b).

Diagram 12
Remove the chenille or slub from the yarn feed and replace it with 'tucking' yarn. Tuck six rows. Change to the first yarn and knit one row, then change back to chenille or slub to knit another row. Continue knitting and tucking, changing the yarns as you do so.
If you like, try varying the number of 'knit' rows and how often you change your two 'knit' yarns. The only thing you must remember is that the number of rows between every six 'tuck' rows must be even, otherwise you could find yourself on the wrong side of the needle bed when it comes to picking up the 'tucking' yarn.
Knit several swatches, varying the number of plain rows between the 'tucking' rows.

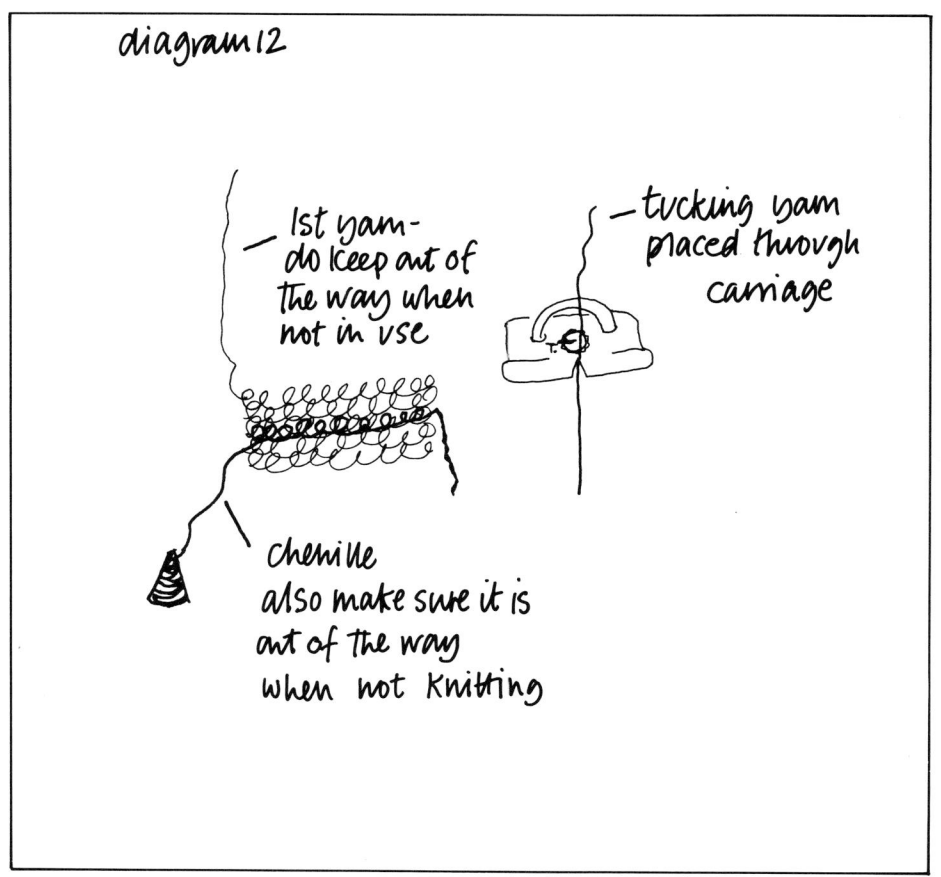

Diagram 13
In addition to the swatches knitted on alternate needles, try one or two using every needle. Use the same punch card locked at the same row, noting that each pair of adjacent needles will tuck, but knit with thinner yarns and tighten the tension accordingly.

Once you are quite familiar with the technique of tucking, knit a swatch on alternate needles to finally establish the yarns and pattern you want to use for your jacket project.

Diagram 14
When you are quite satisfied the fabric is suitable for a jacket, work out the measurements you will need to knit it. The shape is essentially square, as are the pattern pieces and there will be no shaping. You could probably do with a rest anyway after shaping dresses on two consecutive days!

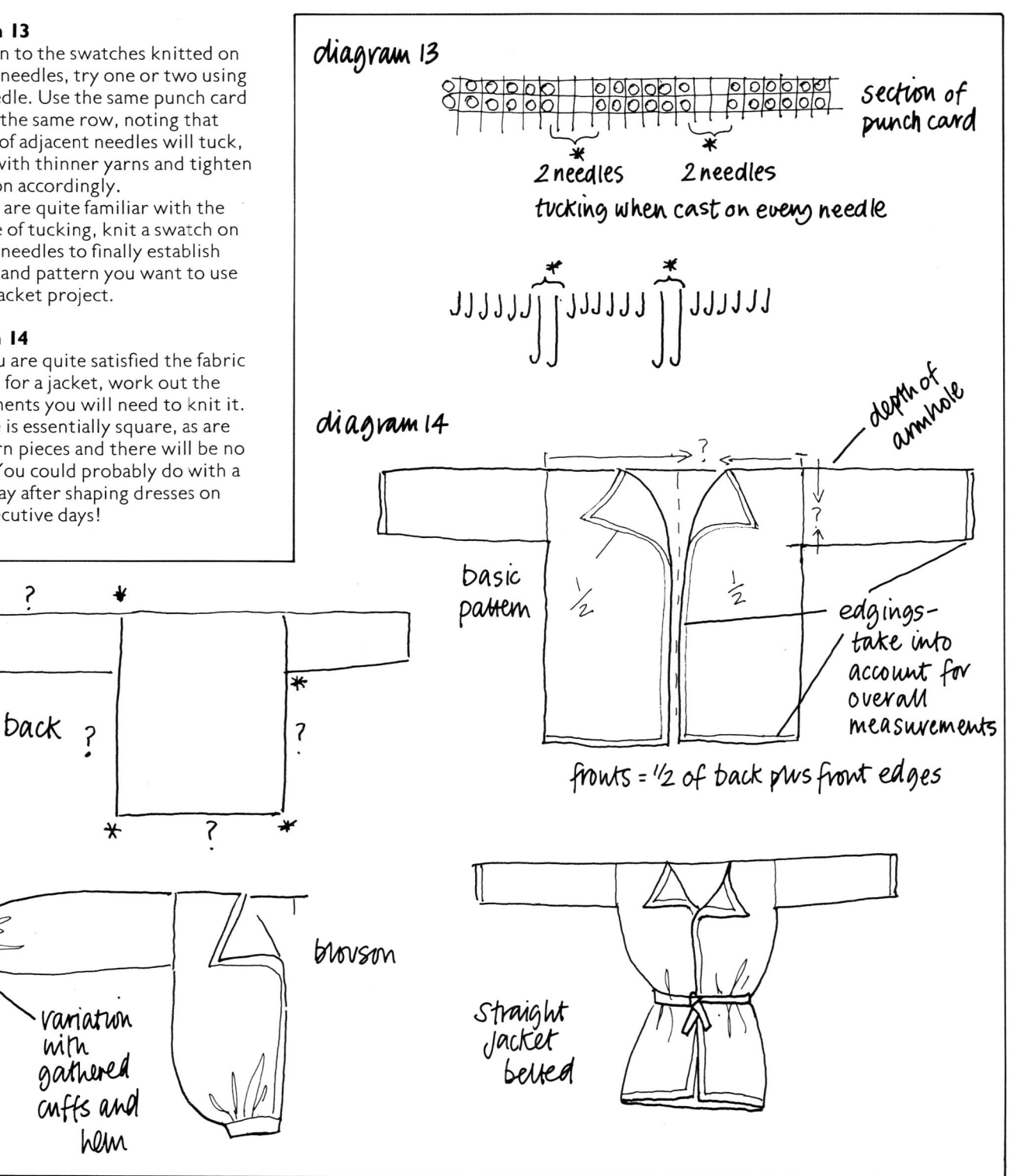

diagram 13

section of punch card

2 needles   2 needles
tucking when cast on every needle

diagram 14

basic pattern

depth of armhole

edgings - take into account for overall measurements

fronts = ½ of back plus front edges

back

variation with gathered cuffs and hem

blouson

straight jacket belted

Diagram 15

With your measurements established before you begin, cast on for the back, knit two rows and attach weights. Continue to knit and tuck until you reach the point at which the armhole begins. Note down the number of rows shown on your row counter and thread a piece of yarn through the last stitch on both sides to mark the row. Continue knitting to the shoulders and cast off. Knit both halves of the front in the same way, remembering to mark where the armholes are.

Diagram 16

Place the front and back armhole rows on to the machine just as you did when constructing Tuesday's jersey, but do not overlap the centre seams.
Knit to the required length.
For the sleeve hems, either make them the same width as the sleeves, in which case knit an ordinary hem, or gather them slightly by placing two or three stitches on to one needle and then knitting the hem. You can also do this on the bottom hem edges.

Diagram 17

Knit the front edges as you did for the bandeau on Monday, and the side slits on Wednesday's dress. Do likewise for the neck of this jacket, making sure you know the width you want before you start.

If you want pockets, knit two squares with hems on the top edges and sew them on to the front of the completed jacket in a position that looks right and feels comfortable. You do not want to have to stretch somewhere near your knees to find your pockets; nor do you want to find yourself fumbling under your armpits for them!
Now that your jacket is finally finished, I hope it proves as useful to wear as it was easy to knit.
Tomorrow, because you have so far concentrated on daywear, and since Saturday is worthy of something a little more glamorous, I am planning that you make an amazing dress for the evening. Though it will certainly be more difficult to make, be assured; it should in no way be beyond your steadily increasing capabilities.

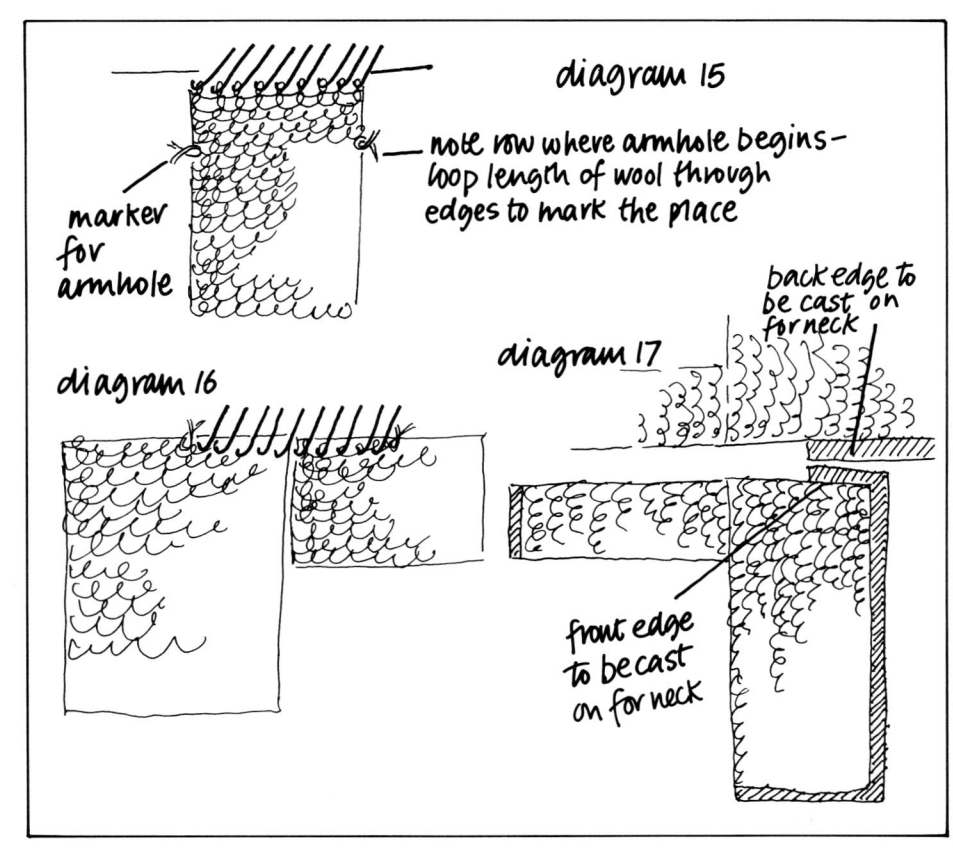

Saturday

At last: the final day of your knitting course. I have planned that you celebrate the occasion by making something to wear this evening – and hopefully it will give you as much pleasure to wear as it will others to look at. I have envisaged this garment as being in black, but it will be as far removed from the traditional 'little black dress' as I can make it. Their only common feature will be that both are predominantly dark; there the similarity will end.

I propose you knit a dress with small cap sleeves and a straight boat-necked top that falls to the hip, which then flares out into a series of fans for a skirt that finishes just below the knee. The neck, skirt and cummerbund will be a rainbow of brilliant colours, and you can then decorate it with feathers, pearls, sequins and any other trimming that will add to its overall extravagance and impact. Do not go mad, however; you could end up with something that looks as if it has come out of a dressing-up box!

First swatch showing experimental stripes in lurex, rayon and chenille

Second and third tension swatch used as basis for the dress

Third swatch showing experimental fan shapes with chenille stripes in-between

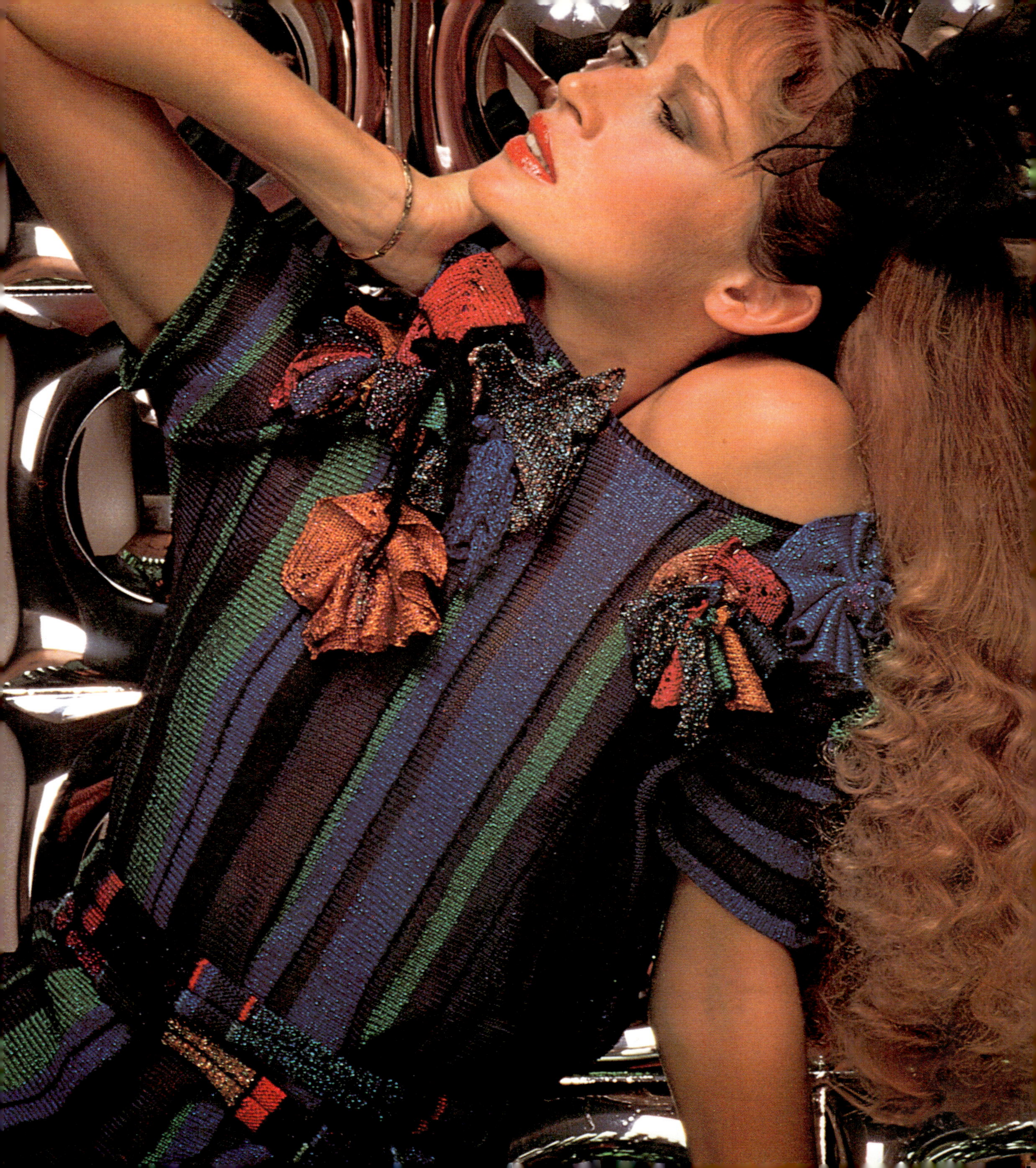

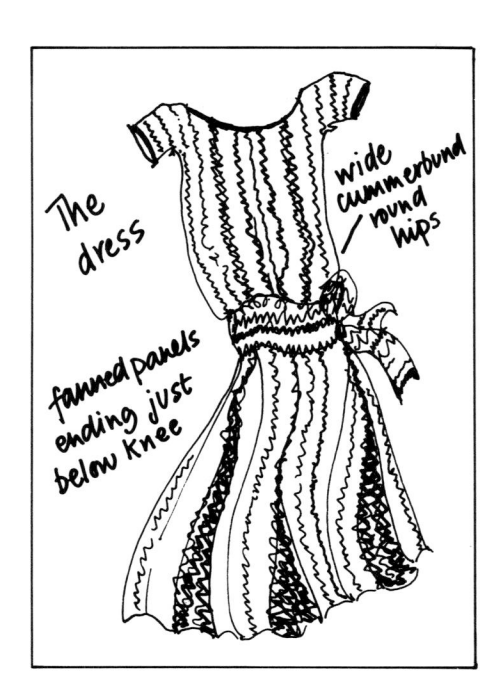

The dress
wide cummerbund round hips
fanned panels ending just below knee

Diagram 1
By now you are familiar with the technique of holding needles. Today's garment uses the same technique to create the fanned skirt that you can see illustrated and in the photograph.
For the first swatch, thread the first yarn feed with your main yarn – the black; then thread the second feed with one of the three brightly coloured sparkling yarns you have chosen.
If the yarns are very slippery and fall off the cone, place a plastic bag underneath the cone to counteract this.

Diagram 2
Once your machine is threaded, cast on as usual and make sure your tension is correct. If it is too loose, the slippery yarn you are using will create an open-weave fabric that you will be able to see through, and when you come to holding needles to create the fans you could end up with a series of very large holes.

Diagram 3
Begin by knitting a series of stripes to familiarize yourself with the yarns, spacing them on the black background for a planned (or deliberately erratic) pattern.
When you decide to change from one colour to another, cut the first yarn close to the cone, tie the second to the loose end and pull the new yarn through the carriage yarn feed so that you are ready to knit with the second colour. Knit two rows (or the required number) and then change to the background yarn – the black – and knit a few more rows.

The yarn you use to knit this extravaganza is, of course, all important. Silk would be the most sumptuous choice, but if this proves too expensive, a good rayon or art silk should work just as well: they all hang beautifully. Rayon, when knitted sideways can sometimes drop unless a stabilizing thread is used; with this style however, this really does not matter.

Next, choose the colours you plan to use. May I suggest two or three brilliant hues for the hems and flares of the skirt – say peacock blue, emerald and orange perhaps – two of which should be either lurex or yarns with a lurex thread running through them. Then select a plain or space-dyed chenille that echoes the colours you have picked.

Whatever your choice, simply make sure the yarns you use are brilliant and glitter so that the effect you achieve will be rich and suggestive of jewels.

Now you have a clear idea of what you are going to knit; but what about actually making it? First, the preliminary swatches.

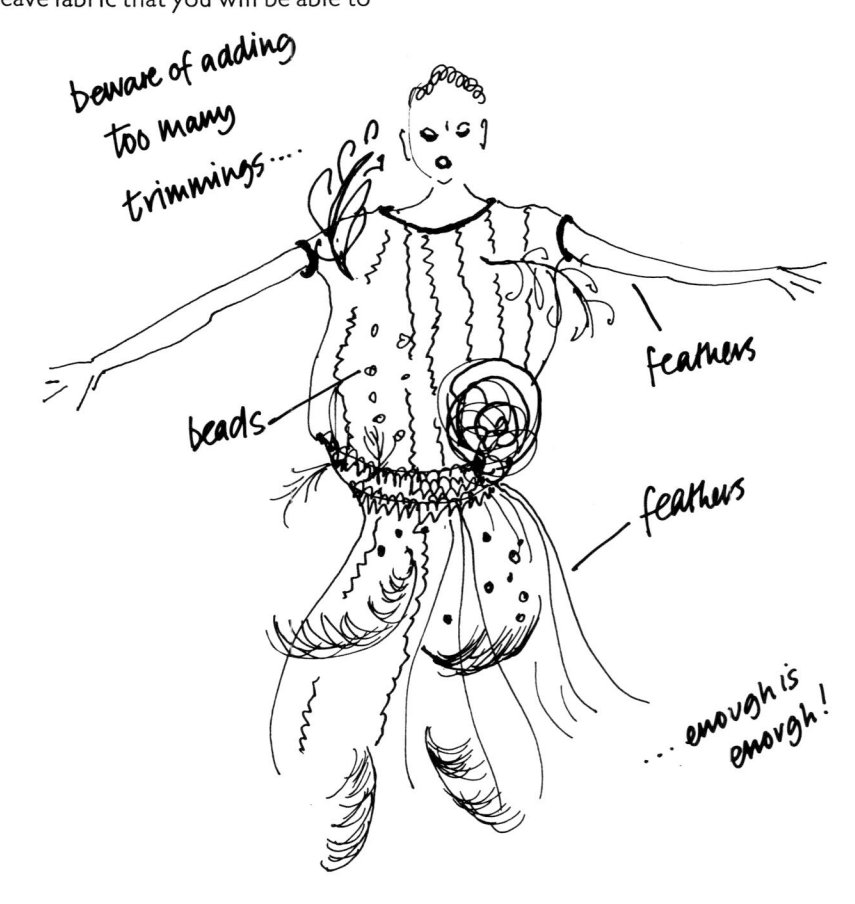

beware of adding too many trimmings....
beads
feathers
feathers
...enough is enough!

Diagram 1
knitted fan

Diagram 2
row where holes are very large if tension too loose

Diagram 3
emerald peacock

emerald
tie peacock here and pull through carriage instead of emerald

Diagram 4
held loosely here

threaded ready for one row of chenille

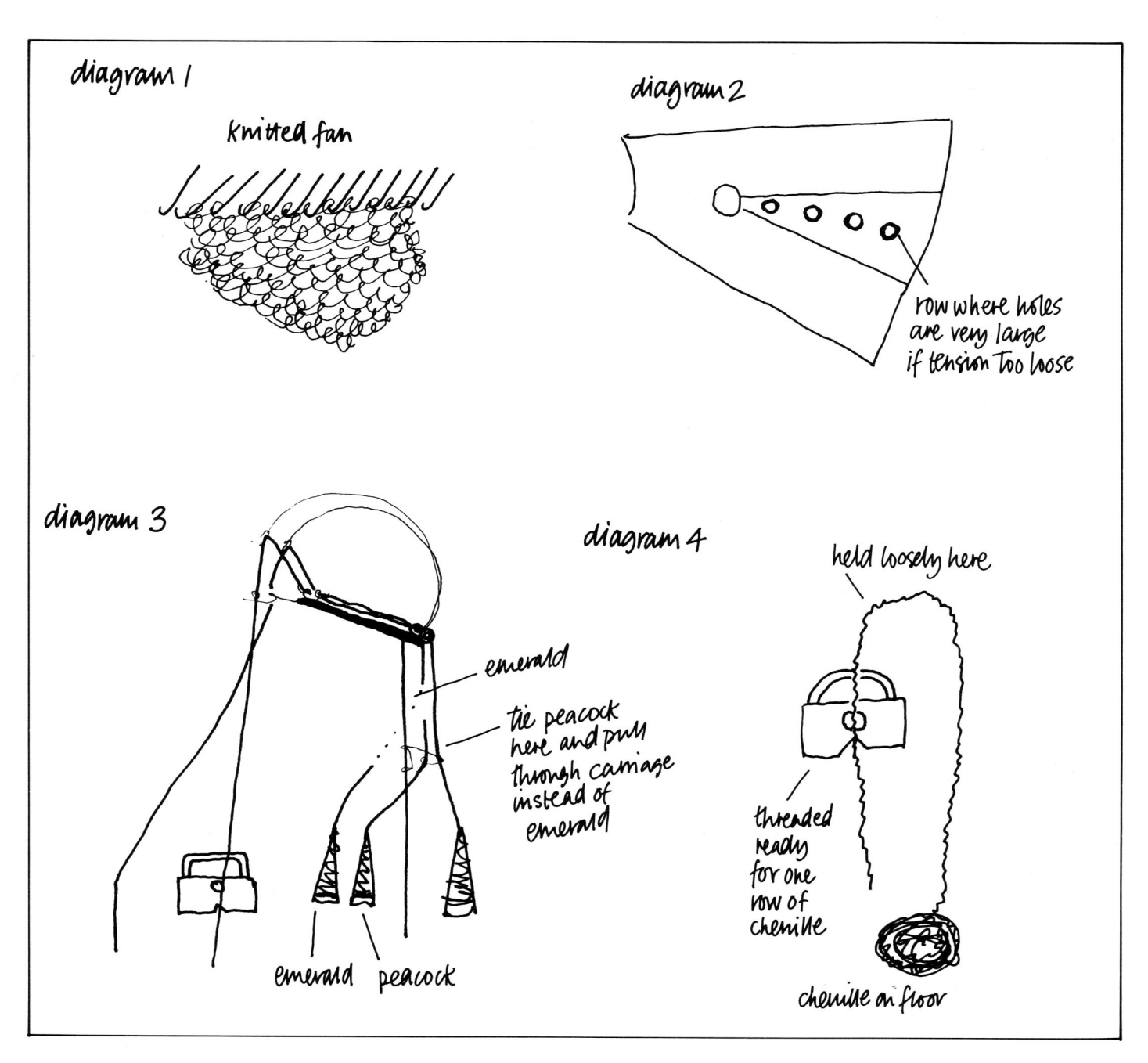

chenille on floor

Diagram 4
After knitting these rows, remove the main yarn from the carriage and, just as you did on Friday, thread chenille through the carriage. Holding it lightly above the carriage, knit one row. Remove the chenille and re-thread with either the main yarn or one of the coloured yarns and continue knitting until you feel like effecting another change.

It is not advisable to knit more than one row of chenille at a time because it is difficult to handle (refer back to yesterday's notes on page 60), especially if the tension is fairly tight. When you have knitted several striped swatches and you feel happy about most of them, you are ready to test the technique for knitting some fan-shaped swatches.

Diagram 5
Cast on as you did for the striped swatches. Knit several rows and then change to a coloured yarn.
Pull, right out, four needles at the side of the knitting furthest from the carriage, then programme the machine not to knit these pulled-out needles. Knit two rows. Pull out two more needles, then knit two more rows (a). Continue pulling out pairs of needles and knitting until all the needles are pulled out (b).

Diagram 6
Now you must repeat the exercise in reverse. This will involve pushing the needles back in two by two, just as you brought them out.
Push in the last two needles on which you knitted; but do not push them so far in that the stitches fall off. Knit two rows. Push in the next two and knit two rows. Continue in this way until only four needles are left in the pushed out position; the same needles that you pulled out before knitting with your coloured yarn.

Diagram 7
Now change back to your main yarn: black. Programme the machine to knit all the needles that are holding stitches and knit four rows.
Now stop.
Look at the knitting hanging from your machine. It should appear as a brilliant section of a circle with a series of holes down its centre, between the two areas knitted in the main yarn. That *is* what it looks like? Good. You can move on now and repeat the fan shape in another colour.
Remember: always knit the same number of rows between each fan section, otherwise the edges of the fans will not be even.
Once you have knitted enough fan sections, remove the knitting from the machine and judge their success. I hope they win your approval!

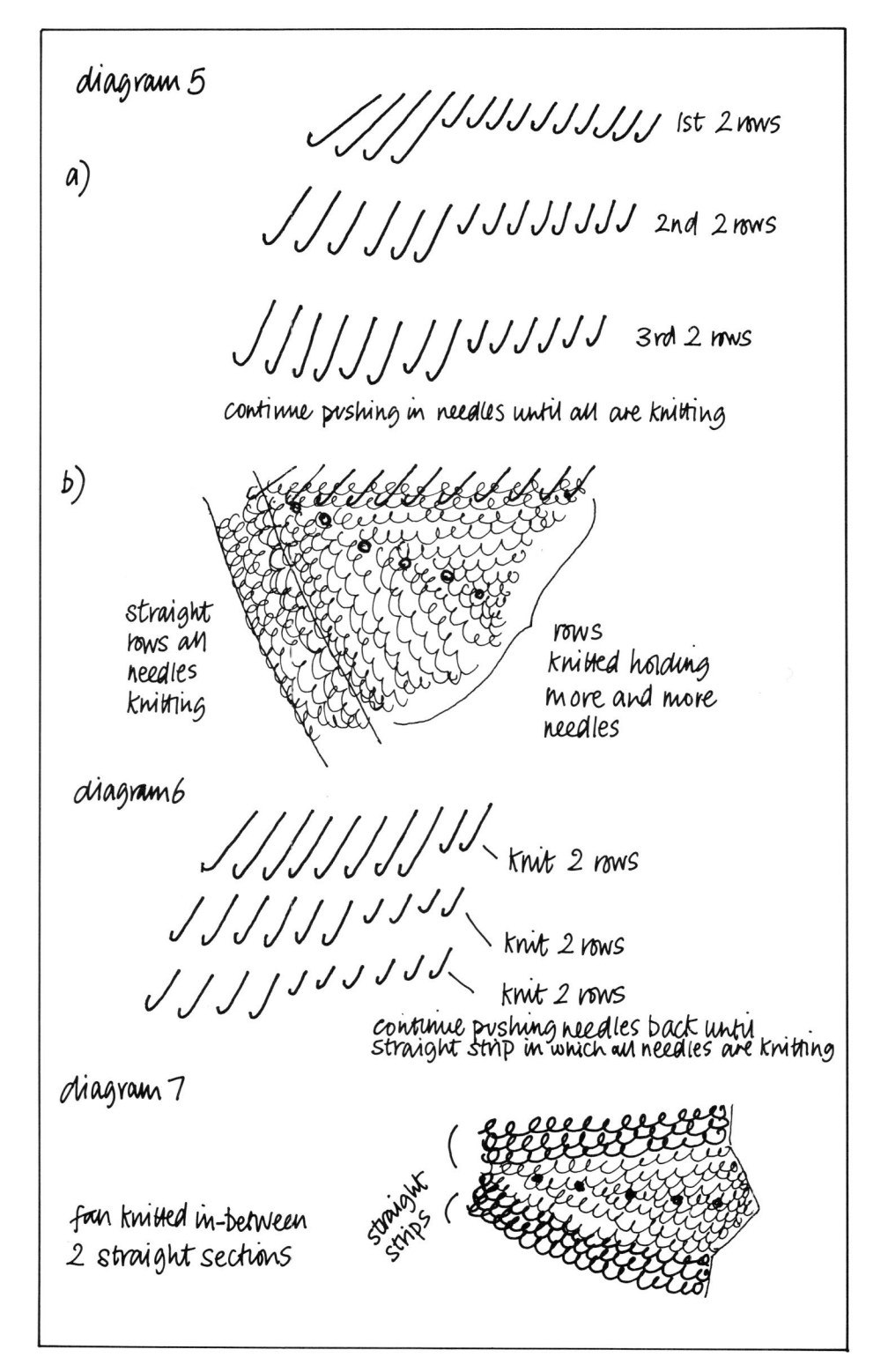

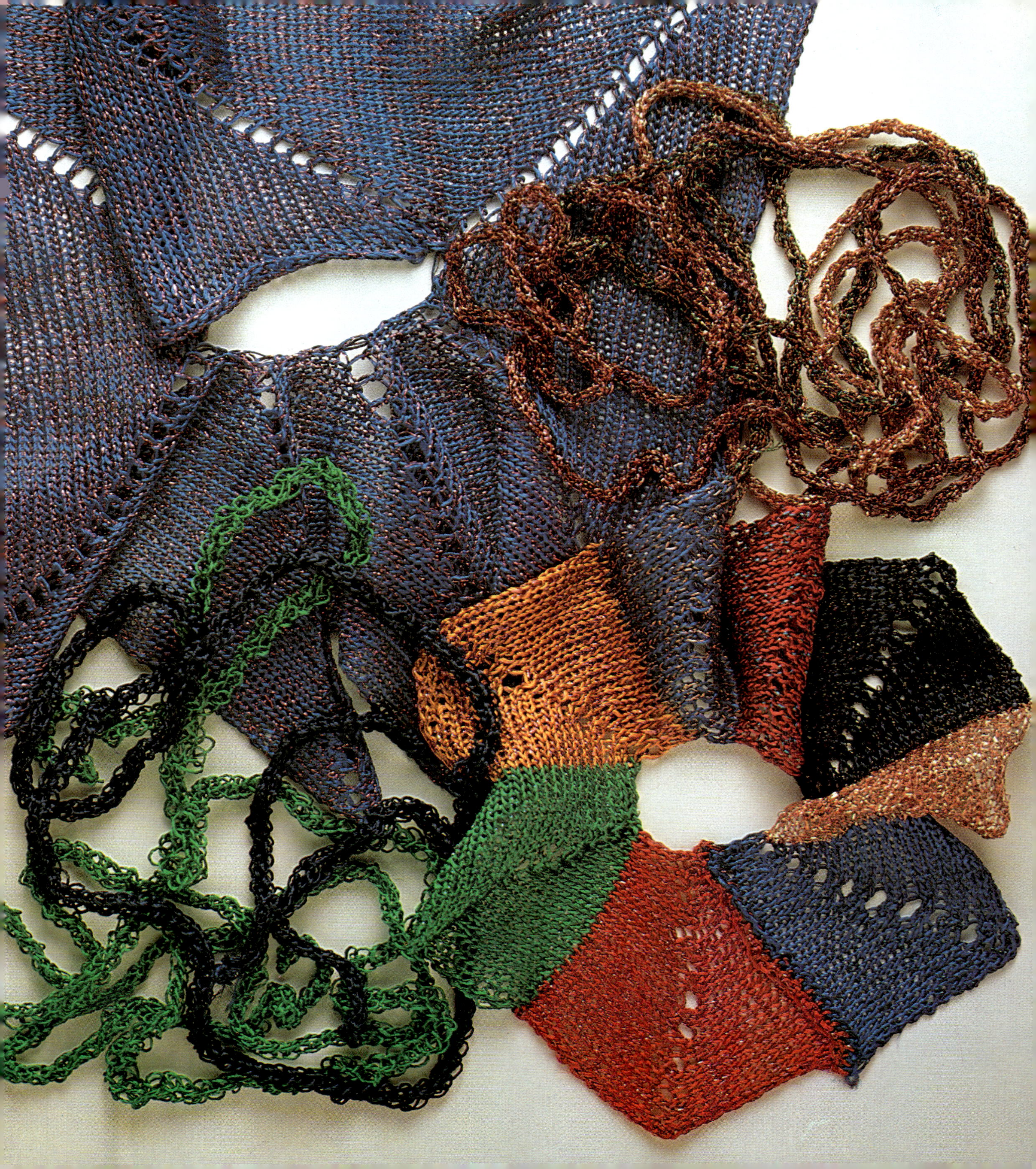

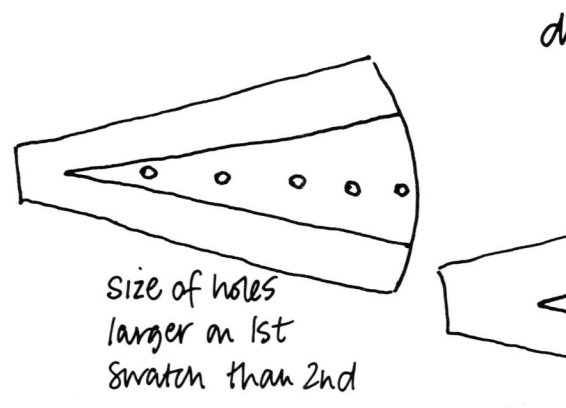

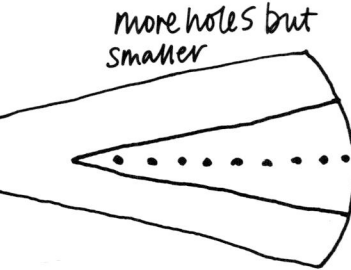

Diagram 8
It is possible that you find the holes that run down the centre of each section a little disconcerting. If this is so, there is a way to avoid making them quite so obvious. Cast on for another swatch and knit several rows in the main yarn. Then bring out four needles at the other side of the carriage as before, knit two rows and then repeat as for the first half of the first section but in reverse (pushing needles in).
Before you knit the first row of the reverse section to create the second half of the fan, push back one needle only to start with. Knit two rows. Then push back two needles and continue until five needles remain rather than four. Now change to the main yarn and knit four rows. You could try wrapping your yarn under the last needle in holding position each time you knit so preventing any holes from forming.

Diagram 9
Compare the difference in the size of holes between the first and this second swatch: although the holes on the second are smaller, there will be more of them.
Having knitted several sections with small holes, with four rows of plain knitting between each, cast off.

Diagram 10
For the next swatch, I suggest you combine stripes of chenille and coloured yarn for the areas between the fans. Instead of knitting four rows in the main background yarn, try one row of chenille followed by two in one of the brilliant colours, followed by two rows of black, and then another of chenille, so making a total of six rather than four.

Diagram 11
You can stripe the fans too. Remember to knit the stripe on the same row coming back, having pushed the needles into knitting position (a and b).

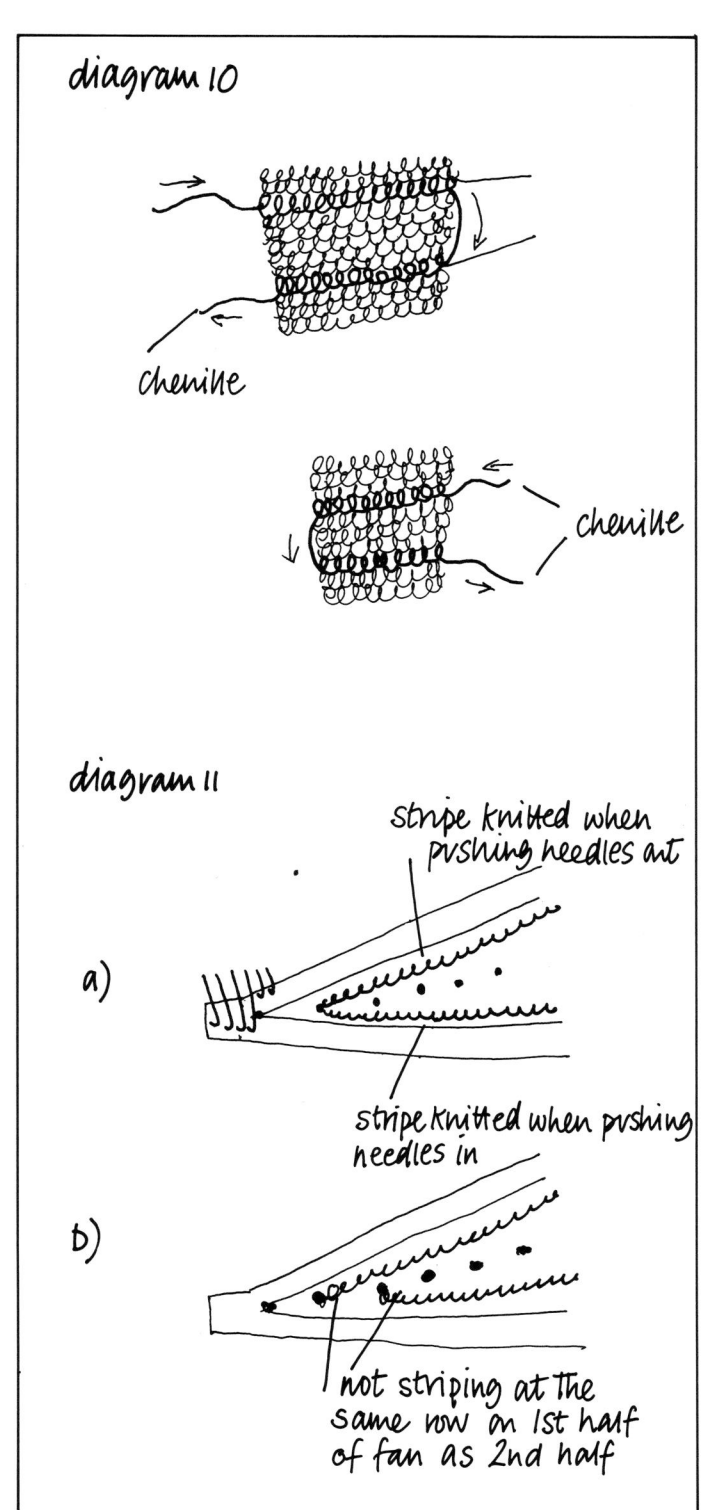

diagram 10

chenille

chenille

diagram 11

a) stripe knitted when pushing needles out
stripe knitted when pushing needles in

b) not striping at the same row on 1st half of fan as 2nd half

The technique has many uses — collars, cuffs, trousers, shirt fronts, dresses and so on ....

Saturday's dress —
fans of lurex and viscose in skirt with chenille and lurex in vertical stripes throughout

lots of coloured lurex, chenille and viscose in gaudy cummerbund — and flowers knitted as rosettes

Diagram 12
By programming the machine to knit on all the needles, you can knit a row of chenille in the middle or two rows using one of the coloured yarns to the total width of the swatch. With this done, change to the yarn you were using for the main part of the fan and re-programme the machine, bringing out all the needles that were out before you knitted the middle row and continue as you would for the rest of the fan.

Diagram 13
One other variation you can make to the fan pattern is to knit a second fan within the main fan section. The principle for this is the same as that employed for the stripe within the section, but instead of changing the colour twice, change it once only (a, b and c).

Diagram 14
By now, you should have a range of striped and patterned coloured fan-shaped swatches. Choose one that is striped on which to base the top of your dress and work out the number of stitches and rows you will need to knit this part of the garment.
Do you remember how Tuesday's jersey was knitted from side to side? You will be using the same technique for today's dress.

Diagram 15
For the front, begin by knitting the cap sleeve and then gradually bring out the needles to shape the sleeve (a) before casting on the total number of stitches for the length of the side (b).

diagram 12

total width of swatch

1 row of chenille

2nd half of section

diagram 13

stripe within section

2 rows change colour
X rows change colour

1st colour

2nd colour knitted until smaller section complete then change back to 1st colour

chenille 1 or 2 rows

diagram 14

cast-off edge

cast-off edge

? rows per centimetre (inch)

cast-on edge

side seam cast on after cap sleeve knitted

stitches per centimetre (inch)

diagram 15

a)

cast on cap sleeve gradually

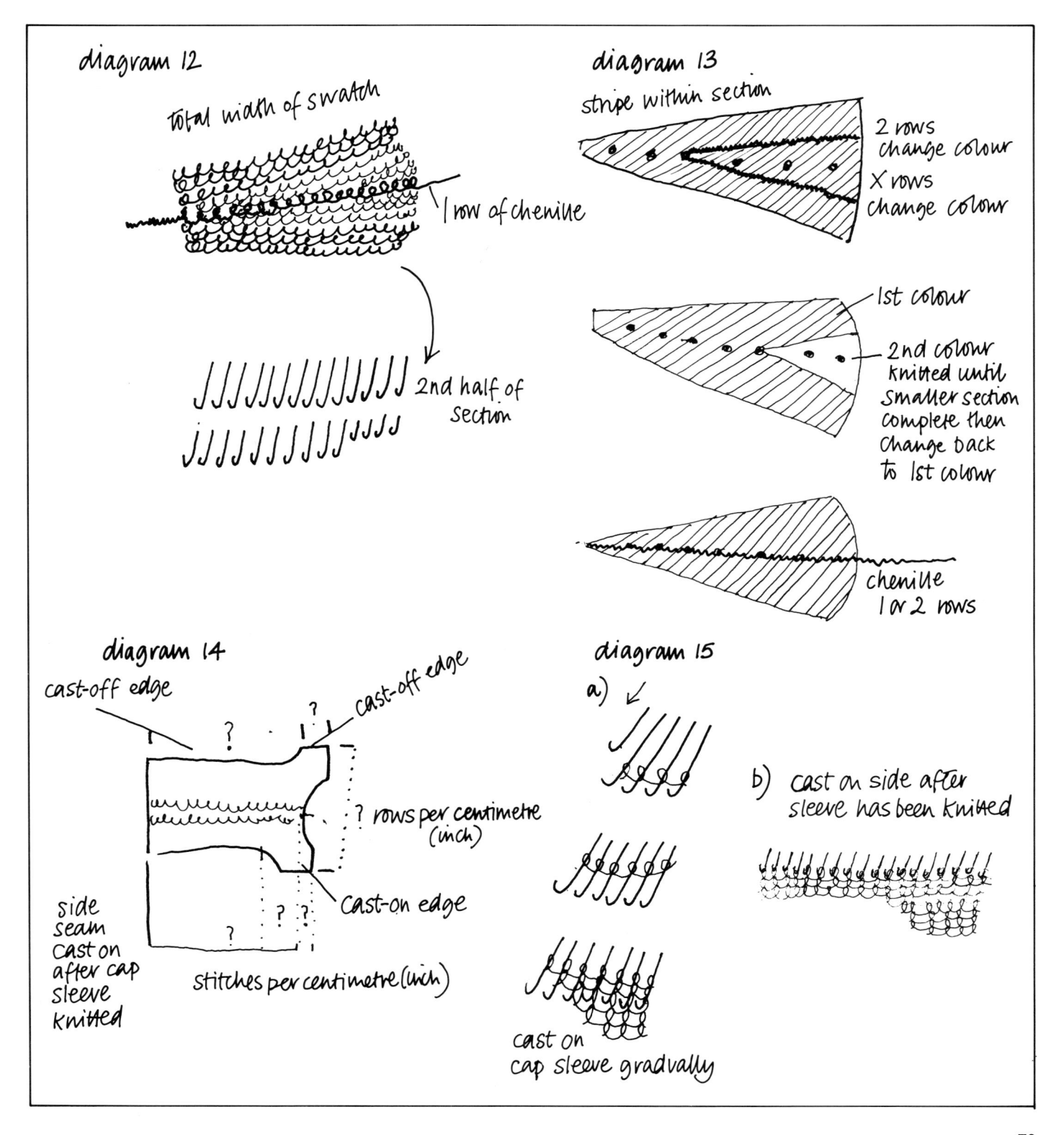

b) cast on side after sleeve has been knitted

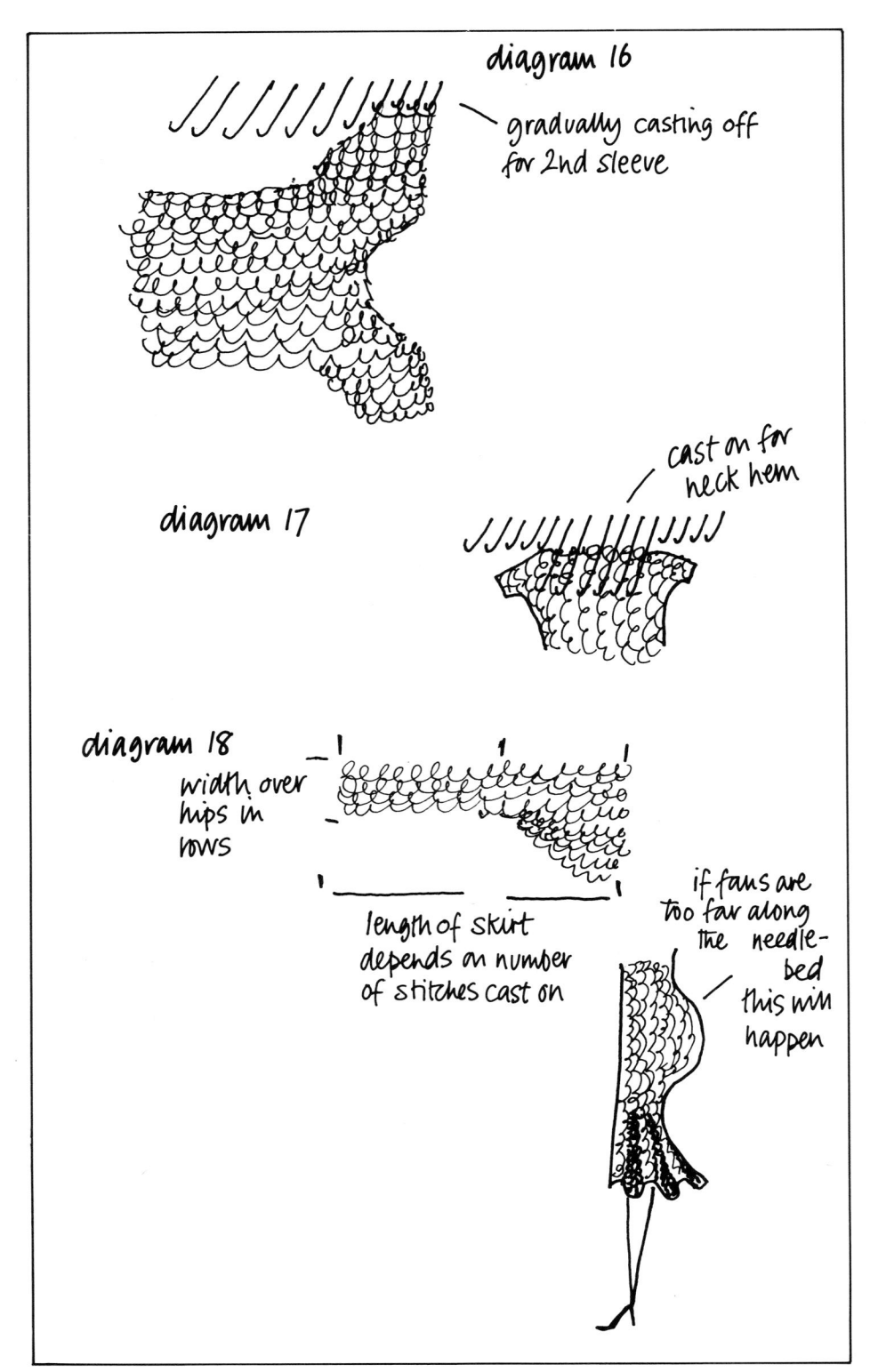

diagram 16 — gradually casting off for 2nd sleeve

diagram 17 — cast on for neck hem

diagram 18 — width over hips in rows; length of skirt depends on number of stitches cast on; if fans are too far along the needle-bed this will happen

Diagram 16
Knit across the width of the top and when you reach the other side, cast off gradually for the sleeve so that it matches the first you knitted. The two must be identical.
Remember also to shape the neck slightly according to your scale drawing, again casting on and off the same number of stitches over the same number of rows on both halves of the neck.

Diagram 17
Knit the hems of the cap sleeves as part of the top half of the dress. They can be striped or plain as preferred. You can knit the striped neck hem once the knitting has been removed from the machine.

Diagram 18
Having knitted the back part of the top to match the front – except for the neckline which will probably be slightly higher – it is time to make the skirt.
Since you will be working from side to side, the number of stitches you cast on depends on the length of the proposed skirt. Also, its fullness will be determined by the number of fans you plan to knit, the number of straight rows in-between each – and the depth of each fan.
Do not begin the fans too far along the needle bed, otherwise you could find the skirt clinging in a most unattractive way underneath your bottom.

Diagram 19
Not only should you space the fans regularly; but they must also be regular in size. Plan one long, one short, one long and so on (a). Avoid knitting one long, one fairly long, one short and another long or the result could be most eccentric (b).

Diagram 20
Once you have knitted the two halves of the skirt, all you have to do is sew in

diagram 19

a) evenly spaced fans

b) unevenly spaced fans resulting in uneven hem

diagram 20

a) striped cummerbund

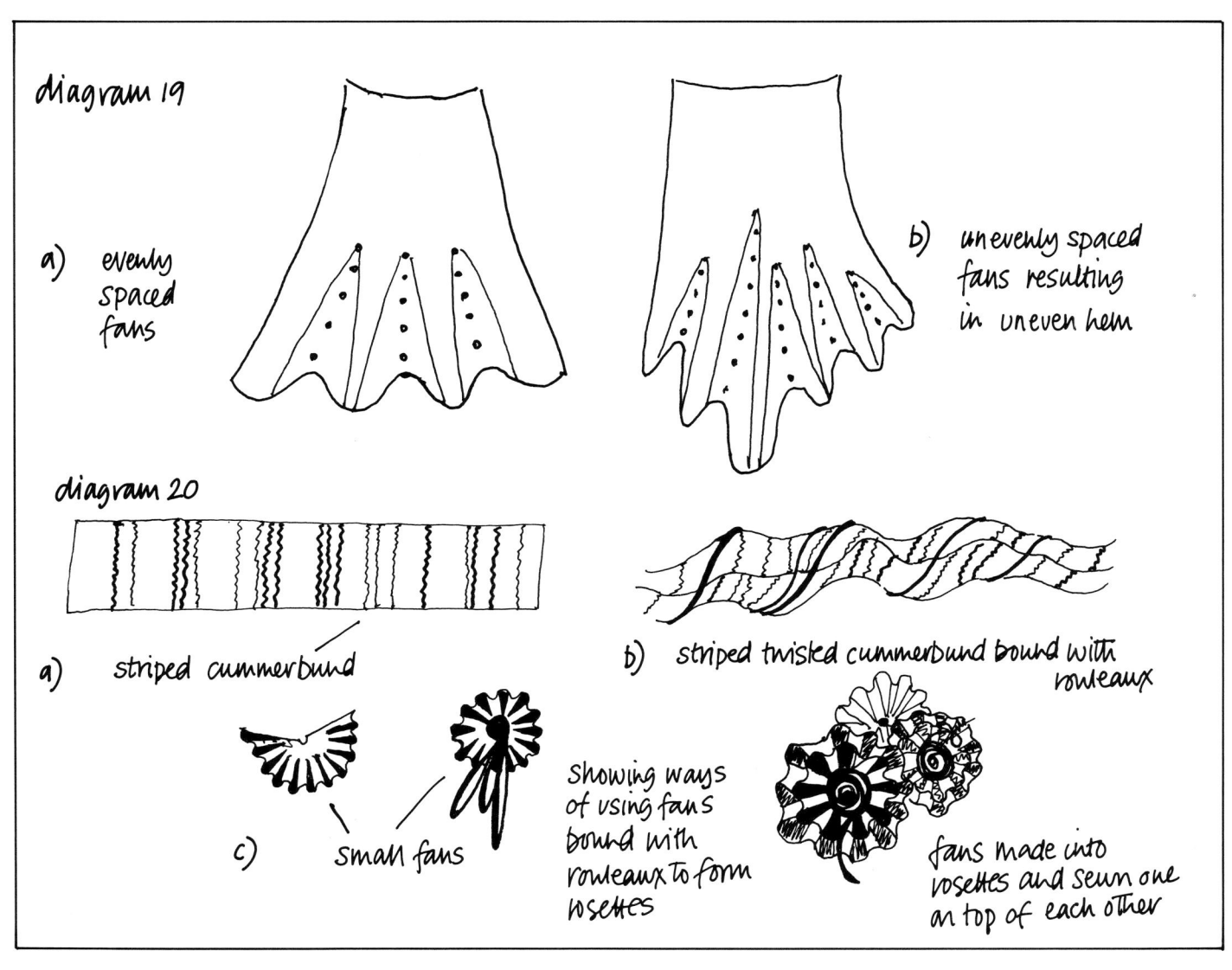

b) striped twisted cummerbund bound with rouleaux

c) small fans

showing ways of using fans bound with rouleaux to form rosettes

fans made into rosettes and sewn one on top of each other

all the loose ends and then assemble the dress.

Now knit an extravagantly striped cummerbund to complement the finished garment, striping it rather more obviously than you did for the body of the dress (a).

If you want to decorate the cummerbund, knit some brilliant rouleaux to twist around it (b); and if you knit some extra shorter rouleaux, try constructing a knitted corsage to wear on the shoulder perhaps, or at the waist.

Finally, knit some small very full coloured fans and gather them into rosettes and tie with rouleaux (c). Once the various details of your dress are finished, you must put it on. It should look very glamorous and quite unlike any other you have ever seen. I hope it makes you feel as good as anticipated! I would be very surprised if it did not. Enjoy the climax of your week's knitting; your dress should last a long time and give you and others a great deal of pleasure – I am sure it will.

Tomorrow, I suggest you give both yourself and your machine a rest. On Sunday, we will be concerned with adding to the techniques and ideas already explained in preceding chapters. It will be a kind of scrap-book and sketch book day filled with interesting, curious and useful suggestions which I hope will prove useful.

Sunday

As I implied at the end of the last chapter, today, Sunday, is going to be very much a day of review and consolidation: an assessment of all the information, facts and techniques so far learned, together with suggestions of ways in which you can continue your exploration of the craft of machine knitting.

I shall be explaining which of the techniques presented so far can be knitted on a double bed machine, which can not, and why. The simplest approach is to discuss each technique day by day and then develop it with an explanation of how the techniques can be enlarged upon in both practical and creative terms.

At the very end of the book, you will find a very useful list of contacts and suppliers that should point you in the right direction for all your future knitting requirements.

Monday

Plain knitting, as you probably know, is otherwise known as 'stocking stitch'. Refer back to one of the early swatches that you made on your single bed machine and you will see that there is a right side which is relatively smooth and a wrong side that is more textured. By programming a double bed machine to knit both beds at the same time, however, you can create a fabric that looks exactly the same on both sides. This is advantageous because it means you can knit a reversible fabric.

Diagram I
You may remember that on Monday I mentioned that it was also possible to knit one bed at a time, so creating a tube or sac the width of the knitting

diagram 1

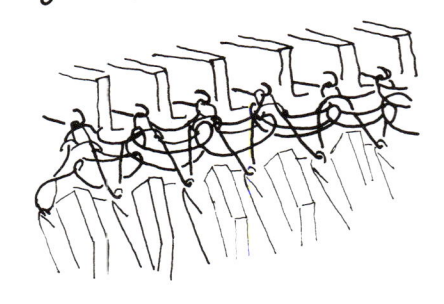

knitting both beds but one at a time.
If you only cast on alternate needles you will create a trellis-like knitting but a loose tension using a fine yarn will allow you to see the material you use for padding through the knitting

diagram 2

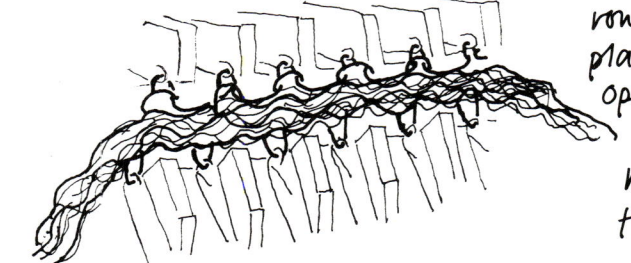

rouleau or roving placed between opened beds in the sac made by tubular knitting and as wide or as narrow as you choose.

By casting on two needles, missing two needles, casting on to two again, missing two and so on on both beds, you will find that your knitting forms a trellis-like sac.

Diagram 2
Whereas you have to thread single bed machines by hand (refer back to your bandeau), with a double bed machine you can simply open the beds, lay in the rouleau, ribbon or whatever threading material you are using, close the beds and then knit one or two rows to seal it into the knitting. Continue knitting and sealing one long sac at a time for what is known as 'tubular' or 'circular' knitting.

Tubular knitting can be padded with many different kinds of materials. For a thick cushion or coat, pad your fabric with wool (or nylon) rovings. These are lengths of wool fibre resembling fat woolly sausages that have not yet been carded and which can be purchased direct from the mill. They will arrive in their natural coloured state but are easy to dye with natural or synthetic dyes. Alternatively pad your knitting with thick twisted yarns, twists of fabric cut to length, ribbons or cords. The material that you place between the beds of your double bed machine will obviously determine the use to which you will put the finished fabric. Knitting padded with rovings or cotton wool will not be suitable for a light top; nor will lightweight knitting threaded with thin ribbon be practical for heavy duty household furnishings. Some of the materials I have suggested laying between the beds of a double bed machine are also suitable for threading through the single bed trellis structure you produced in chapter 1. Experiment with them for interesting and varied effects.

Three padded swatches knitted on a double bed machine - using natural wool roving, dyed wool roving, and strips of shiny fabric

Three swatches knitted on single bed machine using alternate needles, threaded with fabric rouleaux, braids and cords

tied as tight or as loose as you want
loose ends caught in edges of cuffs, shoulder seams and hems – bind with braid, ribbon, petersham or fabric
Rough sketch showing idea for one horizontally threaded top ....
.... and one vertically threaded jacket

Tuesday

The technique you employed for the close fitting jersey in this second chapter was simple enough to learn. It was designed to give you some basic experience of using a wide variety of yarns in combination at different tensions and it knitted into an attractive ridged pattern.

The only real advantage of alternately knitting with thin and thick yarns at various tensions on a double bed machine is that you will produce a reversible fabric, the same on both sides. Here, there is a disadvantage, however, as you will not be able to see and therefore judge the progress of your knitting. I recommend, therefore, that you stay with your single bed machine for this particular ridged effect unless you specifically want the fabric to display the same stitch on both sides.

Since you spent most of Tuesday testing yarns and tensions to estimate which worked best and which could be rejected, I suggest you extend this knowledge by knitting long swatches in virtually every yarn you own. You will learn a lot about the behaviour of different yarns and how they react when being knitted at tensions set anywhere between zero and 10.

Experimental swatch — not all of which worked

- yes — yarn suitable for ridge effect but not enough rows knitted
- too tight tension
- Tension too tight for yarn ridge too hard
- didn't work — no ridges yarns not springy enough
- interesting combination
- dropped stitch

Wednesday

During the making of your multi-coloured tunic dress, I explained how to weave by hand. Here I shall explain how to weave using a much less laborious technique.

Diagram 3
Once you have inserted the punch card, set it to where you want to begin the weaving pattern. Thread the main yarn as you would for plain knitting, setting the tension dial accordingly, then place the weaving yarn through the empty yarn brake and in front of the spike on the side of the carriage nearest the cast-on needles.

Diagram 4
Knit one row, remove the weaving yarn, transfer it to the other spike and knit another row changing the weaving yarn from the left to the right spike for each row. Remember, however, to pull out the first needle on every row so that the weaving begins at the beginning of the row rather than half way along it (a and b).

Try a variety of punch cards to find out which patterns you prefer; some that are good for Fair Isle or Jacquard often prove quite unsuitable for weaving. Alternatively, design your own punch cards for original patterns and effects, taking into account, as before, the practical purpose of constructing the fabric and the use to which it is to be put.

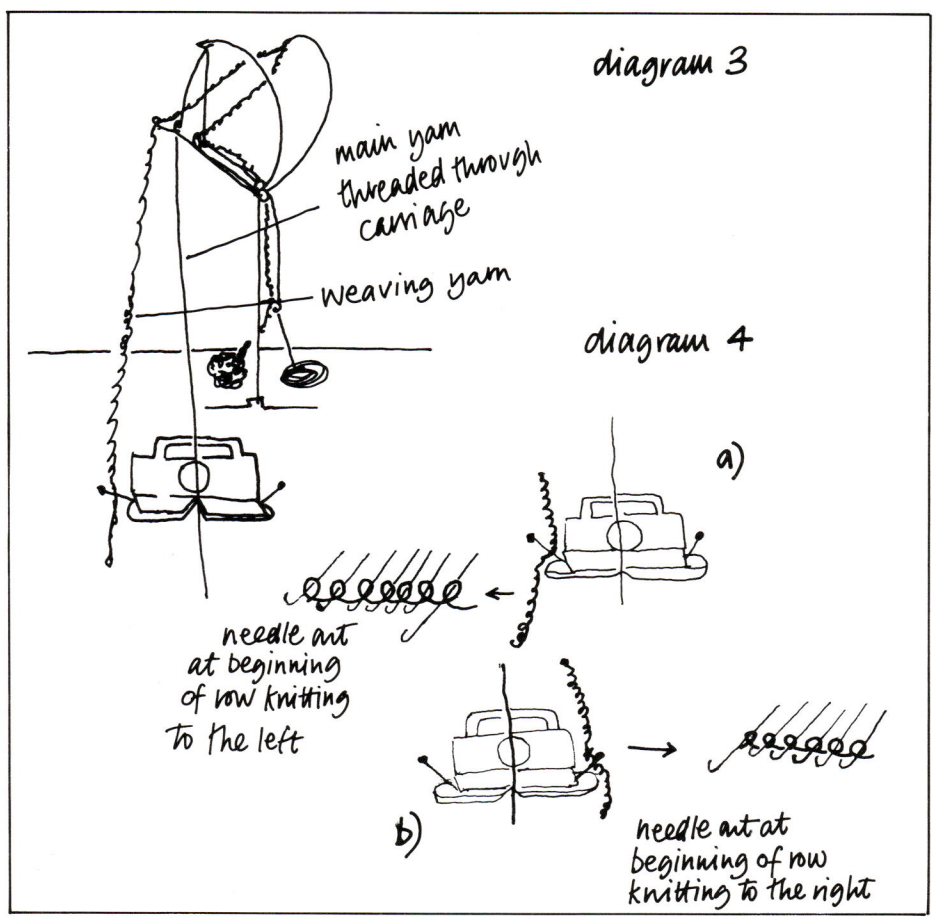

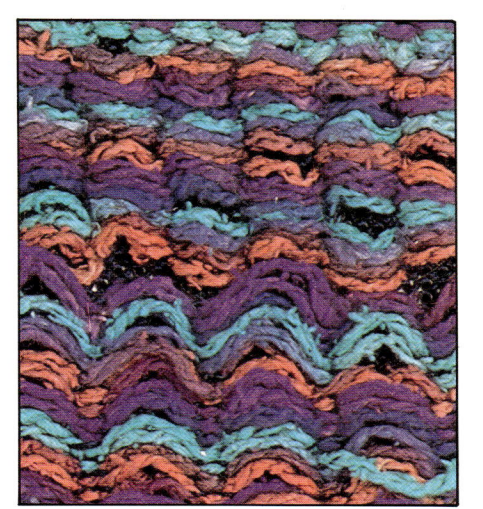

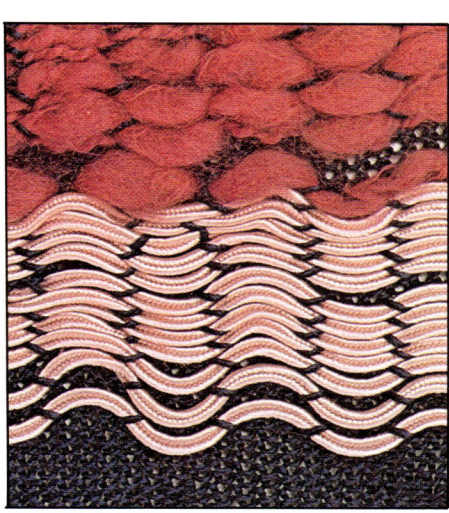

diagram 3 — main yarn threaded through carriage; weaving yarn

diagram 4
a) needle out at beginning of row knitting to the left
b) needle out at beginning of row knitting to the right

Swatch with woven-in space-dyed thick rough silk

Swatch with woven-in cord and thick wool slub

87

Punch card weaving can result in a very warm fabric so making it suitable for winter clothes; or you can knit with very light yarns for purely decorative effect.

Rough ideas for two very large coats: one woven horizontally, one vertically, with woven gaiters to match.

You could also knit a woven muff and a hat....

or, you may just decide to make an extremely warm rug

Two woven swatches using a variety of yarns combining punch card weaving and weaving in by hand. Bright colours on undyed wool background

89

Just as you can use a whole host of interesting materials for threading, so you can with weaving. Experiment with cords, ribbons, lacy trimmings and leather thongs. It seems a good idea to start a collection of possible threading and weaving materials as soon as possible, but make sure they are not too thick or they will prove difficult to weave.

leather strip cut with pinking shears

cord

piping cord

rouleaux

braid

velvet ribbon

go[ld] rib[bon]

Things to use for padding

thick twisted wool roving with fine cotton

wool and nylon rovings

swatch threaded with nylon wool and fabric rouleaux

lurex ribbon

printed ribbon

double bed swatch threaded with silver ribbon

Thursday

So far we have looked at the further possibilities of threading, testing yarns at different tensions and weaving. On Thursday you knitted a smartly patterned Jacquard dress in black and white, and this leads me on to discuss where you should look for ideas in order to begin creating your own designs. One of the problems most commonly experienced is the inability to decide not only on the sort of effect you want, but where exactly to begin. May I therefore suggest that you start by looking at your pinboard where, during your week long experiments, you undoubtedly pinned up all sorts of postcards and objects, yarns and bits and pieces that proved interesting. I am sure that many of these images that initially caught your interest for one reason or another could provide good starting points.

Perhaps there is a postcard, or number of cards, that could prove a useful basis for a design? If not, I suggest you start a collection straight away. In the meantime, I shall assume there is one that suits my purpose: a postcard reproducing a painting or image based on stripes, checks and some kind of formal grid pattern.

Collect a variety of graph papers and any pieces of fabric that seem to repeat the theme in terms of pattern and colour. With all this accumulated material in front of you, study it carefully. Pick out what you like and discard anything that seems irrelevant. Soon the effect you want and can practically achieve should become clear and you can start charting a design on to graph paper. Pin up yarns that seem appropriate and which you can test out in swatch form later on. Of course, it could be that the image that provided your starting point could be translated fairly literally into a design, requiring only simplification. If this is the case, it should be easy to chart and transfer on to a punch card. Having punched your card with the finalized design, it is worth experimenting with different combinations of texture as well as colour. This is easy to accomplish on a single bed machine but rather more demanding on a double bed as, in order to knit a grid, you will first have to mark out the pattern on to graph paper and then push each needle into position as it is required. This is obviously a very time consuming operation and one which I do not recommend. The only real advantage of using a double bed machine for this type of knitting, is that because two beds are knitting, the floats caused by the patterning will be caught into the centre between the two layers of knitting, and therefore will neither be visible or likely to snag.

reverse of double bed Jacquard – no floats

91

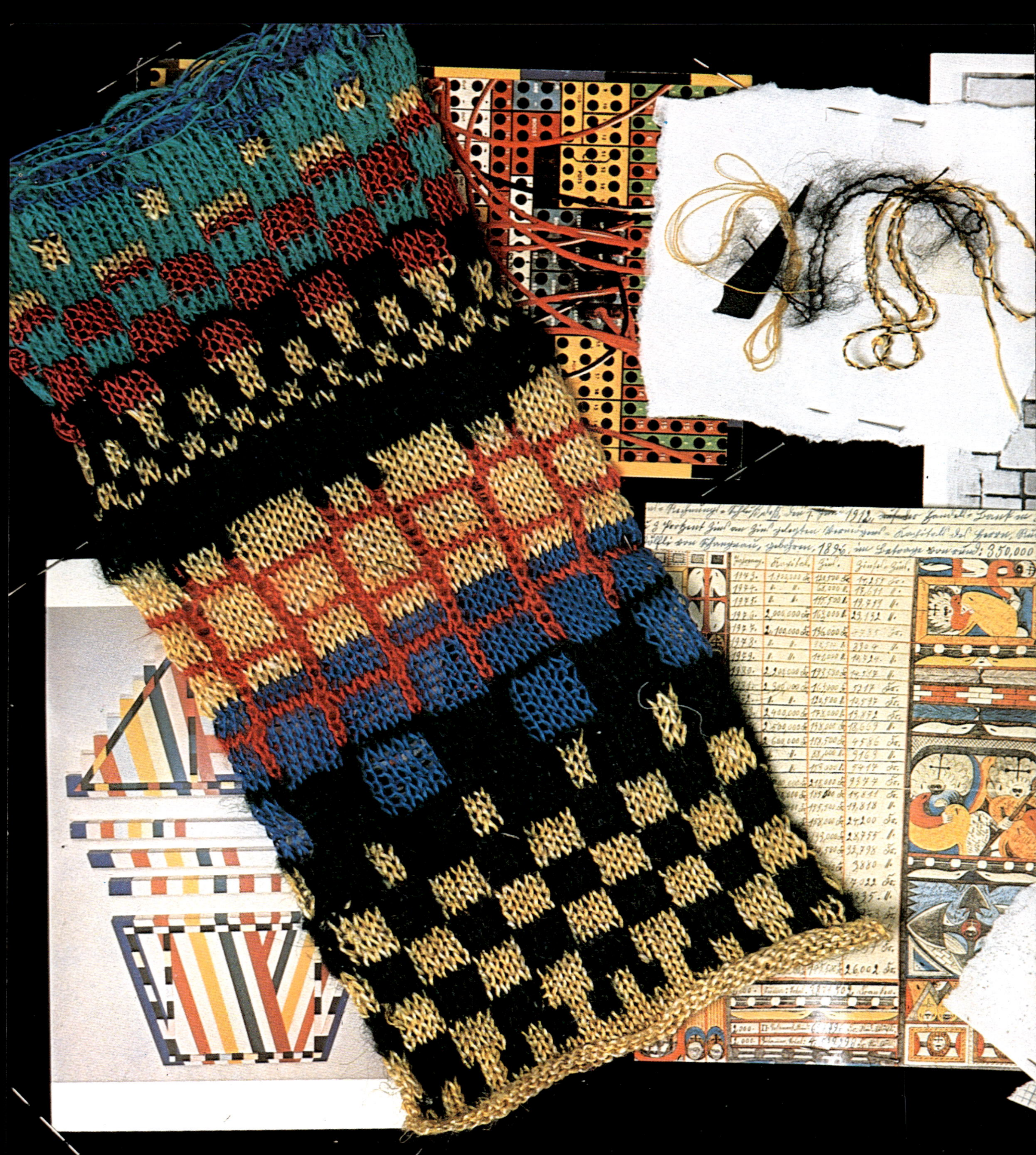

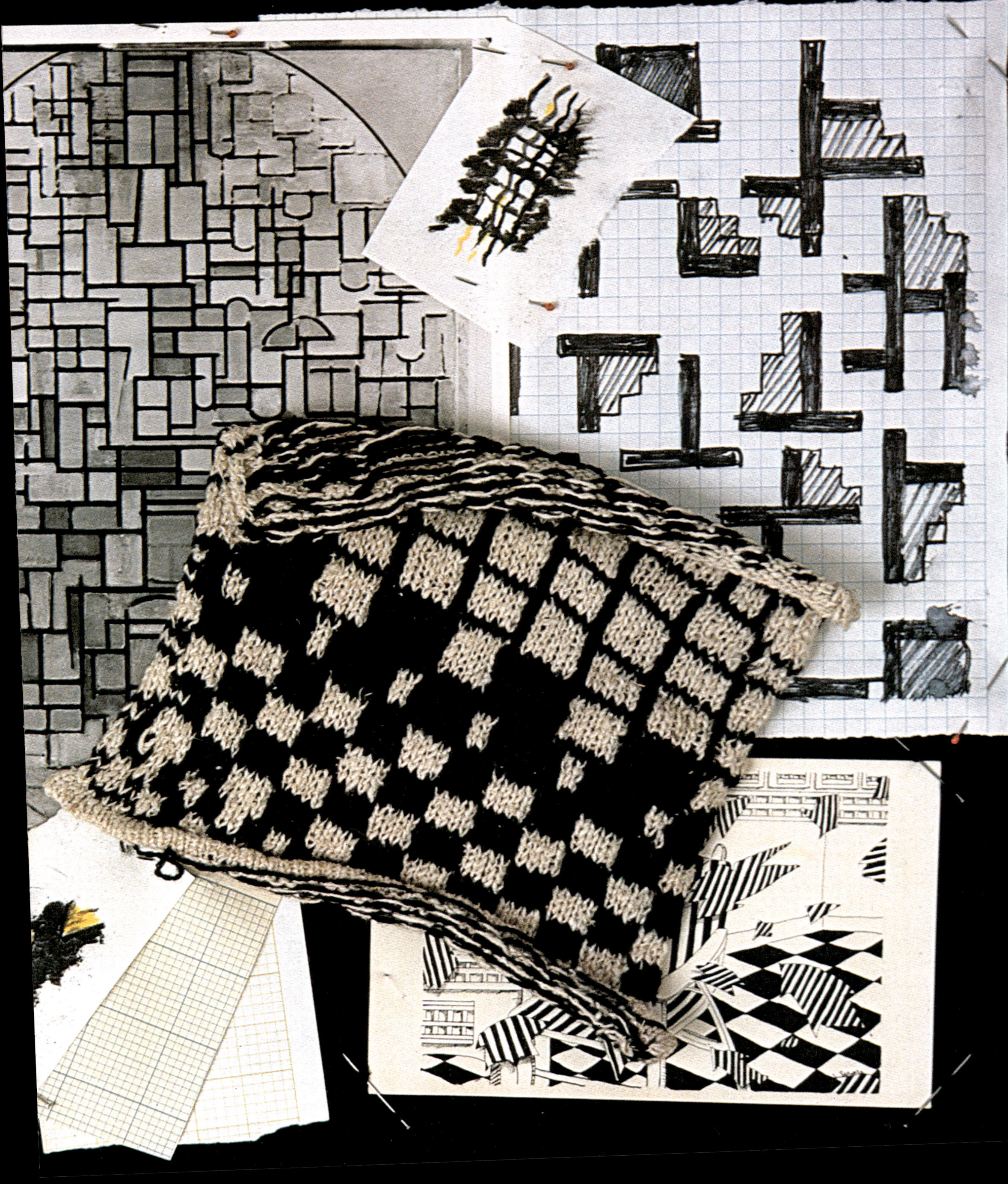

Friday

Towards the end of the week, you learned how to tuck, a technique eminently suitable for a double bed machine. Since there are two beds rather than one, you can tuck either on both at the same time, on one only, partly on one but not the other and so on. As you can see, there are a great number of possibilities.

Diagram 5

If you only own a single bed machine, there is no need to feel limited; there is still quite a lot you can do. For example, tucking with a very fine yarn allows you to tuck a greater number of rows than when using a thick yarn, and this often creates a puckered effect similar to the double bed tucking illustrated (a and b). Another idea to explore is to hold the yarn very loosely and concentrate on the pattern created by the held needles rather than aiming for a raised, three-dimensional effect. This technique produces a lacy fabric which should prove suitable for a soft gathered dress, a blouse or jersey, a shawl, curtains and many other fashion or household items and objects that I am sure you can think of.

diagram 5

a) knitting needles — tucking needles
both beds tucking for 10 rows
knit 2 rows in-between tucking rows

b) back bed holding needles that are not knitting — front bed
needles knitting for 10 rows
tucking for 10 rows
2 rows knitting all needles on both beds

Fine pale yellow swatch knitted in fine yarn on single bed machine using tuck stitch to create lacy effect

swatch knitted on double bed machine. Upper section of swatch tucking as in diagram 5b), lower section tucking as in diagram 5a)

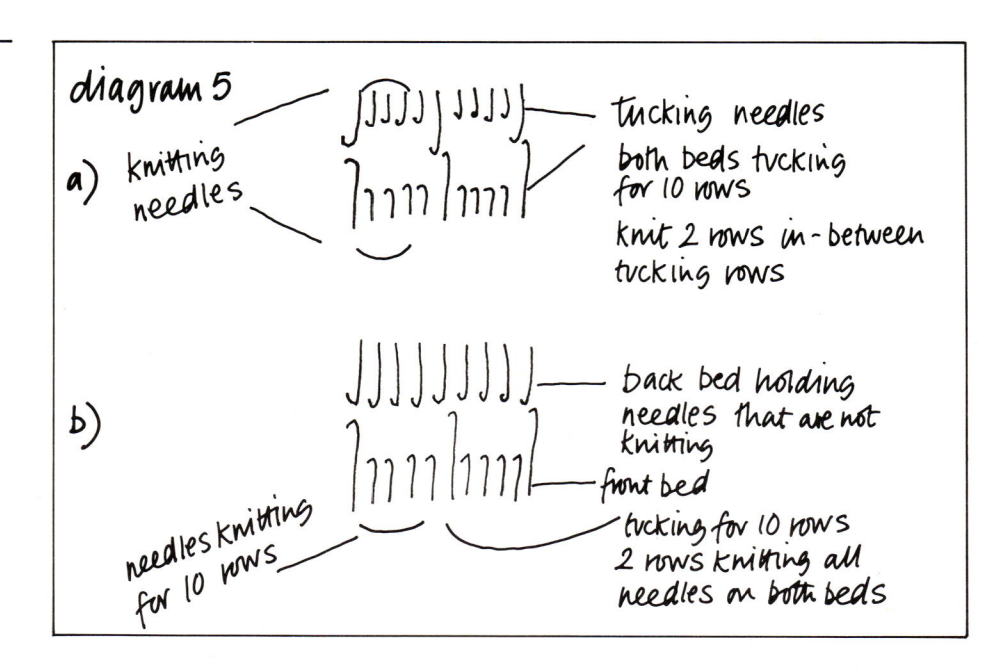

94

Saturday

In knitting swatches for your dress fabric, and making the garment itself, you have so far only experimented with knitting fans in stocking stitch with rows of plain knitting in-between. Why not now try combining fan shapes with woven sections instead? Such a combination could co-ordinate effectively as part of a garment that is predominantly woven; and you can use the same principle with tuck stitch, Fair Isle or simple but effective combinations of different textured yarns. Should you decide to knit a very full fanned skirt, why not decorate it with small knitted rosettes that echo, on a much smaller scale, the colours and textures of the skirt; or if this seems a little 'over the top', wear one in the hair or attached to a wristband as jewellery. Fans are by no means limited to garments and accessories either. Create circles, gather them in the centre and use as table mats; or if you are feeling excessively ambitious and patient, you could knit an enormous circular tablecloth.

Finally, if you want flowers that never die, why not knit some?

By now you will have realised that there are an infinite number of things you can knit, even within the limitations of the single bed machine; and by purchasing a double bed to supplement your first buy, you will be equipped well enough to knit yourself an almost completely knitted environment.

I will leave you, therefore, with the thought that whereas only a theoretical seven days ago you were a complete novice who found the idea of trying out your machine rather daunting, this is no longer true. You now control your machine; not the other way around.

I also hope that the confidence you have gained and the techniques you have tried and tested will enable you to use it over and over again with ever-increasing enthusiasm and that there is never any possibility of your machine finding its way under your bed or to the back of a cupboard to gather dust. If this is so, and your wardrobe is soon bulging with original designs that express every single emotion and mood imaginable, this book will have achieved its aim.

95

Useful information

Knitting Machines – a selection

Knitmaster
Knitmaster Ltd, 30-40 Elcho Street, London SW11
Basic machine is the model 120 plus ribber and accessories; single bed models 260KL and 360 are one-action lace makers which can be adapted to double bed machines; one-action electronic model SK600; foldaway model MK70.
Comprehensive service includes:
School at Elcho Street; knitting clubs throughout the country; home tutor service for purchasers; tuition tapes; after sales service; regular newsletter; pattern service; company is always willing to give advice by letter or over the phone.

Passap
Bogod Machine Company, 50-52 Great Sutton Street, London EC1
Swiss-made machines, distributed in Britain by Bogod, who also distribute Bernina sewing machines; knitting machine range is basically double bed, in four versions; attachments can be added to the basic model to make up any of the three more advanced versions, or each version can be purchased complete; basic model consists of double bed and stand with two-colour changer; additions include: four-colour changer, automatic punch card pattern unit and motor.
Services include:
Over 100 stockists, each with trained tutors available to instruct in the shop or in the home by arrangement; every purchaser is entitled to a free course of instruction in the London office. Additional courses are also run in London at a cost of around £12.50 per day; two or three model books containing patterns are published every year.

Singer
Knitting Machine Dept, 255 High Street, Guildford, Surrey
Single bed punch card model KE2600; ribbing attachment KR13, comes complete with four-colour change attachment; electronic model 2310.
Services include:
Lessons free from all Singer shops; pattern catalogue in all shops from which patterns can be ordered; Singer 'Hot Line' advisory service.

Toyota
Aisin (UK) Ltd, 34 High Street, Bromley, Kent
All machines are single bed: automatic punch card lace knitting machine 747; ribbing attachment 450; super automatic model 901 and ribbing attachment 501; plain knitting machine 510.
Services include:
Tutors all over the country go into purchaser's homes at nominal cost; knitting school in the Kent office; pattern service.

Jones/Brother
J + B, Shepley Street, Guide Bridge, Audenshaw, Manchester
All machines single bed: current models include KH830; KH840; KH860; KH710; KH881 with built in knit leader; electronic KH910; KH230 with wide gauge for bulky knits; ribbing attachments available.
Services include:
Some dealers give free tuition; J + B have their own demonstrators in large department stores across the country; magazine, 'Stitch in Time'; always happy to give information and answer queries.

Yarn Manufacturers – a selection

Patons
Consumer Liaison Dept, Messrs Patons and Baldwins Ltd, Allca, Clackmannanshire, Scotland
(Wide range plain and fancy hand knitting yarns, some of which are suitable for machines.)

Robin
Robin Mills Ltd, Idle, Bradford, West Yorkshire
(Plain and fancy hand knitting yarns. No machine yarns in their range.)

Emu
Emu Wools Ltd, Leeds Road, Greengates, Bradford, West Yorkshire
(Plain and fancy hand knitting yarns. No machine yarns in their range.)

Hayfield
Hayfield Textiles Ltd, Hayfield Mills, Glusburn, Keighley, West Yorkshire
(Plain and fancy hand knitting yarns, some of which are available on cones for machine knitting.)

Lister
Lister-Lee, Whitecak Mill, Wakefield, Yorkshire
(Plain and fancy hand knitting yarns. Machine knitting range is a 4-ply called Thermo-knit.)

Sirdar
Sirdar Ltd, PO Box 31, Alverthorpe, Wakefield, Yorkshire
(Plain and fancy yarns for hand knitting, some of which are suitable for use on machines. No yarns are available wound on cones or sold specifically for machine knitting.)

Specialist Yarn Suppliers – a selection

All the following companies offer mail order facilities:
Bulner and Lumb, Buttershaw, Bradford, West Yorkshire
(Nylon tops for padding.)

T. M. Hunter, Sutherland Wool Mill, Sutherland,
(Shetland knitting and weaving yarns)

J. Henry Smith, Park Road, Calverton, Nottingham
(Cones of yarn for machine knitting – a very good selection)

Shaw and Marvin Ltd, Station Road, Beeston, Nottingham
(Cotton and acrylic yarn merchants)

William White and Sons, Whitehall Mill, Leeds Road, Huddersfield
(Mercerized cotton, silk, rayon, synthetics and many other fancy yarns)

William Hall and Co. (Monsall) Ltd, 177 Stanley Road, Cheadle Hulme, Cheshire
(Processed and fancy yarns)

Learning about machine knitting

Part-time courses
London: Adult Education Institutes all over London offer Creative Machine Knitting courses. For details, see 'Floodlight', the ILEA guide to part-time day and evening classes or phone ILEA Information Office.
Outside London: phone local education authority information office or contact machine manufacturers and dealers; their trained instructors may be willing to give additional lessons.

Full-time courses
Three-year full-time or four-year sandwich courses are available at the following Polytechnics in Textile/Fashion or Textile Design. All include the design and production of knitted fabrics leading to BA(Hons) or BSc(Hons).
Birmingham, Brighton, Bristol, Huddersfield, Kingston, Leicester, Liverpool, Middlesex (chief study is offered in woven textiles and knitted fabrics), Manchester, Newcastle-upon-Tyne, Preston.
Trent Polytechnic in Nottingham offers a four-year sandwich course in Knitwear Design BA(Hons); also courses in Fashion BA(Hons) and Textile Design BA(Hons).
For further information see prospectuses for individual polytechnics.

Magazines

'World Wide Machine Knitting', Springvale Estate, Cwmbran, Gwent, Wales
Published monthly; order through local newsagent or contact above address.

Fashioncraft, 48 Buckingham Palace Road, London SW1
Published monthly; generally available or order; two machine knitting patterns per issue.